Without Fear

By the same author
Beating Aggression
Survive the Nine to Five

With Pamela Nottidge:
Slimnastics
Stress and Overstress
The New Penguin Slimnastics
The Whole Person Approach to Fitness

With Kate Frost:
Body and Soul

Diana Lamplugh OBE

Without Fear

The Key to Staying Safe

OLD BAKEHOUSE PUBLICATIONS
─────── FOR ───────
THE SUZY LAMPLUGH TRUST

First published in Great Britain in 1991 by
George Weidenfeld and Nicholson Limited,

Re-published for The Suzy Lamplugh Trust in 1994
by Old Bakehouse Publications.

Copyright © Diana Lamplugh 1991

Published by Old Bakehouse Publications,
Church Street, Abertillery, Gwent NP3 1EA
Telephone: 0495 212600   Fax: 0495 216222

British Library Cataloguing in Publication Data
Lamplugh, Diana
   Without fear.
   1. Self-defence
   1. Title

613.66

ISBN 1 874538 25 5

The right of Diana Lamplugh to be identified as author of this work has been
asserted in accordance with sections 77 and 78 of the Copyright Designs and
Patent Act 1988.

Printed and bound in Great Britain by
J.R. Davies (Printers) Limited

This book is dedicated to GEMMY
(and my husband Paul)

It cannot be often that a dedication is made to a horse. However, without her three bounding leaps after emerging from the high bracken into the gorse on a wild Welsh mountain, I would not have injured my back so badly that the resulting enforced rest would enable this book to be written. Of course, I would rather have done without the pain but the time was invaluable.

My husband, Paul, is the real hero; his care, concern, constant interest and amazing enjoyment of his new role as 'carer' and culinary expert has been the greatest blessing I could ever be privileged to share and enjoy. Our lives are a true partnership through which we hope others can benefit.

The Suzy Lamplugh Trust

The Trust was founded on 4 December 1986 after the complete disappearance, now acknowledged almost certainly as murder, of Suzy Lamplugh, when about her normal daily work as an estate agent.

Since then the Trust has raised awareness of the problems of aggression and violence and has changed attitudes, with the object of enabling people to live safer and enjoyable lives.

The Trust's work is preventative: a positive reaction to the aggression and violence which in its many forms seems endemic in society today.

The Trust stimulates and works with the establishment, the authorities and relevant agencies to search for answers and provide practical help for everyone.

It provides personal safety leaflets, books, videos and personal alarms; training manuals and talks and courses throughout the country; education for children.

Its campaigns for changes in the law and procedures include campaigns for safer mini-cabs, safer car parks, trains and stations (Diana Lamplugh is a member of the British Transport Police Committee), for treatment of sex-offenders so they are not released to re-offend, for a co-ordinated policy for missing persons (the Trust set up the first helpline for relatives of missing persons) and for more help for victims generally.

All the Trust's work is based on research.

The Trust's concern is for the safety of everyone. Living through a nightmare and experiencing the heartache enables us to look clearly at what, for many, is a very murky ground.

The Trust is not government funded and needs donations to continue its projects for the personal safety of everyone.

Acknowledgements

The Appendix lists the many sources on which the statistics and safety guidelines are based, among them the Home Office, the Metropolitan Police, the Department of transport, and Health and Safety Executive and many more. I would especially like to thank the Home Office for their cooperation on the statistics.

I am especially grateful to Inspector John West of the Metropolitan Police who helped with many of the statistics and comments.

I am also deeply indebted to the consultants who have given freely of their time and expertise to go through this material with a red pencil:

Tony Black, Clinical Psychologist; Mental Health Act Commissioner.
Fiona Brown, PR Consultant, Chatto.
Supt. Paul Mathias, Metropolitan Police.
Liz Potter, Social Worker and mother of teenagers.
Lily Seggerman-Peck, Sociologist.
Dr. Joanna Shapland, Criminologist at the University of Sheffield, Centre for Criminology and Socio-Legal Studies.
All my other teachers and students from whom I learn every day.

Diana Lamplugh OBE

Contents

Confidence begins with being aware of the reality of the problem and the potential risks any one of us might face. In this chapter we examine the historical, social and cultural reasons why our perception may differ from the facts. We also consider the width and depth of the definition of aggression as well as the gender differences.

The understanding of stress and tension is a fundamental start to helping you to face problems as well as to learn new skills, tech- niques and strategies which will help you deal with, defuse and avoid aggression. Practical ex- ercises will help you control reactions and cope with confidence in difficult circumstances. Long term advice enables you to achieve your full potential.

Strategies to avoid aggression and becoming a victim of violence are always the first choice before attempting heroics. Assessing, reassessing and reacting to instinct are essential in helping you to be aware of danger points in your daily life. Anticipating and recognizing a risk, then taking action is a practical formula applied to your home, being out and about, on public transport and at work. Being with others as members of a group or team will allow those strategies to be practised and asserted by others.

This chapter looks at all aspects of communication; verbal, non-verbal and emotional as well as 'distressing communication' such as sexual and racial harassment. Basic assertiveness techniques help us to get our point across to avoid misunderstanding and conflict. Learning to say 'no' is especially useful if we are not to raise aggression in others.

Being aware of potential aggression is an important factor in recognizing and responding to a real threat without fear. Knowing when and how to mediate; or protect yourself from attack is crucial to confidence. How to use physical restraint but only as a last resort.

Foreword

This book is written for *you* – whoever you are; young or
mature; male or female; going out to work or working at home.
Everyone who wants to stay safe should know what is in this
book.

It has never occurred to me to want to write a best-seller
before but now I am determined to do so. Not, I hasten to
add, because I want to make a personal fortune – all the
royalties will be ploughed back into the work of The Suzy
Lamplugh Trust which works in the fields of personal safety
and freedom from aggression and violence; the problem of
missing people and their relatives and friends, as well as for
the treatment and sentencing of sexual offenders, aiming to
reduce the numbers of offences and the traumas to the
victims. The reason I want you to read all this commonsense
is because I have begun to realize that commonsense is so
very rarely common practice.

My first book on this subject *Beating Aggression – a Practical
Guide for Working Women* was also published by Weidenfeld
and Nicolson in 1988. I wrote it with the help of a number of
experts in the subjects covered. The book is still valid and I am
told very useful indeed. However it has two constraints. The
first is that it is specifically aimed at women and the next that
the subject matter appears to be confined to the workplace.

Having now given so many lectures, talks and training days
to such a vast number of people, I realized that I must have an
extension of that book if I am to reach the people who most
needed to hear, understand and put into practice the 'Safe
Sense' we were preaching. Men were embarrassed to buy a
book which made it clear that it was for women, and certainly
that applied to young men, who were in fact the most at risk

and the least cautious. And yet when they took part in the training or talks they were enthusiastic and even slightly relieved to be able to discuss the actuality of the problems they were having with aggression, even violence, and not feel their masculinity was being threatened.

Parents, girlfriends, wives all told me how their men had been mugged, '6ft, strong and not a fear in the world and yet he was done over', was a confession I heard often. People said they felt safe in their cars and yet our research showed this to be a high-risk area. The elderly dreaded going out at night but most attacks take place late afternoon with the combination of energetic gangs being let loose from schools, and lunchtime pubs closing with the effects of low-blood sugar after boozy, high protein/fat lunches which can make anyone bad tempered.

The average person's chance of being a victim of any kind are very low – your chances are once in a hundred years! However some of you work or live in difficult areas and many of us face problematic situations. All of us run risks at sometime or other. This book will give you the information on which you can make your own much more informed decisions.

I think perhaps it might be salutory to bear in mind that my daughter Suzy's disappearance made headlines and continued to do so for years. If her case had not been so extraordinary it would not have received so much attention.

However it disturbs me to find that in the 'Missing Persons' part of the Trust we can always get publicity when girls are involved but rarely for young teenage boys. Yet, these are in the majority and, we feel, the most at risk. While the media still concentrate on the female angle the true perspective of the problem will remain distorted. The same happens in the matter of aggression and violence with the result that men lack understanding and women can be stigmatized as victims and too vulnerable to employ in the work for which they are best suited.

It is time we faced with clarity the reality and the answers. The aim of The Suzy Lamplugh Trust is for you to *Stay Safe*, in order for you to be able to do this you need the ABC of Safe Sense

Actuality – Anxiety
Building out Problems
Body Language
Communication
and
Confidence

Protecting yourself can be as straightforward as ABC – Take Care by forming your own Safe Sense Action Plan.

Diana Lamplugh
Spring 1991

Introduction

The alert sounded with the first phone call: 'Do you have any idea where your daughter might be Mrs Lamplugh? We wondered whether she could have called into home for lunch?'

For lunch? Why on earth should she do that? I had in fact asked Suzy to come to lunch on the Wednesday. I had planned a small party of friends for my fiftieth birthday. I hoped she might join us. Suzy had flatly refused – her boss was a stickler for time, she could never make it there and back within the hour she was allowed by the Estate Agents for whom she worked as a negotiator.

This was Monday, it was now about four o'clock, why was her manager ringing me? 'I don't want to worry you, Mrs Lamplugh,' he continued, 'but Susannah left to show a house to a client just before lunch and she has not returned, we just wanted to check everywhere we could.'

It was so unlike Suzy, who usually stuck to the rules and regulations – something must have gone wrong. I said: 'Have you checked the house; perhaps she's got locked inside? Has there been an accident? What about the hospitals? Perhaps her car has broken down?'

He promised to ring me back and did so an hour later. 'We've tried to find her everywhere,' was the message. 'Ring the police,' I said – and then left alone I was immediately struck by total shock. I tried to phone my son, I could not recall the number or even see the written entry in our telephone book; I could not leave the house, I could not scream, my brain had seized. I began to stagger around in a helpless daze, waiting for my husband to come home from work.

It was only later that evening that my initial reaction of

frozen shock gave way to a flood of adrenaline which shot me into overdrive. We must find her; physically all that energy must be directed into *action*. My husband and I went down to the river to where her car had been abandoned. We called, we shouted, we encouraged our dogs to search for her. It was now the middle of the night. We must have been disturbing the neighbourhood but, more than that, as the police who were there made clear, we were getting in their way. Our tracks were crossing any that might have belonged to our daughter, our dogs were getting in the way of their dogs.

We had to return home. We had lost our beloved eldest daughter and as day followed day, weeks, months and then years, there has been not a single trace of her. Nothing. Just as though she has been erased by a rubber.

I was trapped in the house. At the time I was a teacher in Adult Education, and a founder and active director – teaching teachers – of a nationwide health-related fitness association. It was my holidays and that very Monday we had started a huge re-building, re-decorating project on our home. Three of our four children had left home and we had at last begun to feel we could start to flap our middle-aged wings. This had been my summer project. And now all was chaos.

The building work continued; the air was always full of falling plaster dust, the furniture upside down, the carpets rolled up, wires hung from the ceiling, new central heating pipes leaked. We moved our bed from room to room, eventually sleeping in the sitting room and also eating and working there, and from there giving interviews, both radio and television in our bid to find Suzy. My husband had to go back to the office but my work had changed. Every part of my body, each shot of adrenaline was now aimed at finding Suzy and what had happened to her.

I was not alone, apart from the builders and marvellous friends and neighbours, the house was filled with journalists. It did not take me long to learn that the media under certain circumstances make very good pupils! Together with the police, we sought ways that might 'flush out the hare'. Sadly it did not work, our combined talents never bore fruit – but they did highlight many gaps and grey areas and these led to the foundation of the Trust which we set up in our daughter's name.

How could someone as lively, healthy, fit and streetwise as Suzy become the victim of abduction, assault and, as eventually acknowledged, murder. Gradually I began to listen to the journalists as well as answer their questions. 'I got into problems once,' they would tell me. 'I was held in a lavatory with a knife against my throat,' 'He shut the door and I was trapped,' said others.

Slowly I began to realize that Suzy had made some very real and disastrous errors. It also became apparent that any one of us – male, female, young and old – could also, just as she did, walk straight into such a problem without a second thought.

* In the first place, Suzy only wrote down the man's name ('Mr Kipper') not his address or telephone number, nor did she ring back to ensure that the man was the man he said he was. If she had done, she might well have discovered that he was using a mobile phone from the local wine bar from which he could see her in the window and see when she picked up his call.
* Secondly, no one saw this man. She did not bring him into the office and introduce him to the receptionist, effectively both logging herself and him in and out. Not seeing him ensured no one could give a description or recognize him again.
* Suzy had told us that someone had been pestering and following her. Her office staff too, although they knew of the calls which had annoyed her, had not heard his voice. Suzy told us the night before she disappeared that she thought she would have lunch with the man (who she did not name) and make it clear that he was to get lost. But she countered my, 'Don't you think that will escalate things darling?' with, 'Oh Mum, *I can cope!*'
* That's what we all think, when it comes to it, that we 'can cope'. Even though as Suzy also said to us, 'I do find him scary!' she pushed aside this intuitive warning with the

innocence so many of us carry around – it will not happen to *me* – others fall foul of unpleasant problems but somehow we believe ourselves to be infallible.
* The last mistake Suzy made was so simple that I am sure any one of us could have done it. Suzy allowed her social behaviour to take over in the workplace. She allowed a man, she found scary, who no one had seen, who had pestered and annoyed her, to show her into a house which she knew was locked, with windows barred, the electricity turned off and telephone removed. She walked straight into a trap. It was an instinctive reaction that the man had relied on and was said to have used many times before.

With hindsight, it became clear to me that these errors could have been prevented by personal awareness and active procedures worked out by employers and employees working together to ensure everyone's safety – combined with training to guide people towards awareness, their own likely reactions and choices, and avoidance techniques, leading to safety rather than confrontation. When I really looked at it, I realized these precautions applied to everyone, whether at work or leading their daily lives.

At the time I wondered if I was over-reacting, an over-wrought mother thrashing around for some explanation for the loss of her much-loved daughter. Because I was already in the business of running conferences, workshops and training courses, I gathered together all the experts I could find to discuss my thoughts; to ask the question, 'Is there a real problem of personal aggression and violence?'

'There certainly is,' came back the answer from the police, the psychologists, the employers, the media. But this was just verbal admission, we needed statistics. *Elle* magazine did a survey which more than underpinned all our thoughts, and we went on to full-scale research by the London School of Economics sponsored by Reed Employment.

I began to shout out for answers and they came in; university studies used one theory, trainers put forward another, psychologists had other ideas. Looking at these different skills, techniques and strategies, I realized that they were all useful; interwoven they became the key to confidence and the personal management of aggression. This was beginning to be very exciting: like a jigsaw, filling in pieces, they made a whole.

We then invited the various experts to come together at the House of Lords to give presentations. This was the occasion when I realized that essentially I had got it all wrong!

I had thought we were talking about attack and rape. I had to understand that aggression and violence was *much* wider than that. We also had to include verbal abuse, harassment, bullying, innuendo and even deliberate silence. All these forms of personal assault are debilitating in themselves and can also escalate into real threat, confrontation and consequent danger.

My second mistake was to believe that this was a gender problem. Brought up on the theory of the female being the weaker sex, fuelled by the stereotypes of society, reinforced by my own personal experiences and the emotive stories in the media, I jumped to the conclusion that the message which came from Suzy's tragedy was that of a true nightmare of a hidden reality. I had proved myself to be as innocent as all those journalists. The reality is quite the opposite.

The aim of this book is to guide you towards:

- recognizing the many guises of aggression and violence
- assessing the risks
- knowing your own abilities
- realizing your strengths
- accepting your responsibilities
- being aware of potential problems
- responding to a real threat

This book is not intended to be a 'Do as I say – or else' statement. On the contrary, the objectives are to present you with practical knowledge and things which you can do which will enable you to assess your abilities so that you can make

'Informed Choices' armed with the awareness of the possible consequences of your decisions.

Confidence in yourself comes from being aware of the reality and knowing that you can draw on and put into practice techniques, strategies and skills which will enable you to manage, defuse and deal with aggression and even violence.

This book is not intended to scare you into not going out – to make you a prisoner of your fears. On the contrary, it will give you pointers as to how to develop your own skills so that you can lead a full – and a safer life.

Assessing Personal Risk

The fear of becoming a victim of aggression or violence can be a very real problem for some people. This is particularly acute if you live in a high-crime area, have already been a victim, or feel that there is little you can do to prevent yourself from becoming a victim.

Fear of crime can be made worse by the way that the media reports some crimes. It is an emotive subject; violent crime against an elderly person receives full media coverage, as do sexual crimes, thereby giving the impression that they, the people concerned, figure highly as a victim group, whereas the opposite is true.

We will look at the actuality of crime and determine the most and least prevalent of crimes. We will discuss the facts and examine whether our perceptions of crime are correct.

We will try to begin to understand the misconceptions.

At the end of this chapter you should be able to:-

- have a knowledge of recorded crime statistics
- be aware of the emphasis placed upon emotive crimes by the media and the reasons for this
- be aware of the actuality of prevalent crimes compared to the fear of less prevalent crimes, and be able to see these in perspective
- be aware of how history, society and culture has shaped our thinking and our actions
- be prepared to acknowledge that the management of aggression is a people problem – not a gender issue!

The idea behind this book is to enable you to gradually eliminate the risks you can personally run of becoming a victim of aggression.

* The first step is to look at the *Actuality* – the statistical chances of you personally becoming a victim and to understand what we mean by aggression.
* The second step is to learn to cope with our *Anxiety* and the tension and stress this can cause.
* Next you can take some practical actions and *Build out problems* where we live, when we travel, or are at work.
* Then you can learn more about *Body Language*, how it affects you and how you affect others.
* Now you can think about *Communication* techniques and how you can defuse aggressive situations.
* All these will give you *Confidence*. This in itself acts as a deterrent and will help you avoid and deal better with problems and even cope with violence and emotive aggression.

If confidence begins with being aware of the reality then it makes sense to start with looking at the actuality of the potential risks anyone of us might have to face.

The Home Office study on the fear of crime and other studies show that the perceived level of crime sometimes bears little resemblance to the true level of crime, particularly crimes of sex and violence.

Fear of becoming a victim is a very broad and complex issue but it is important because it relates closely to your quality of life. It is very understandable that some people are afraid. Going out alone after dark in a dilapidated inner-city area bumping into groups of people who have been drinking; exposure to media reports of horrendous rapes and murders: all these and many other things may induce in you or reinforce your fear of crime.

What crimes should we be concerned about, what crime are you most likely to be a victim of? (Remembering, of course, that this will depend to a certain extent, on your lifestyle.)

You will see from the pie chart opposite, which represents nearly four million crimes, that the most likely crime that will happen to you (or someone you know) is connected to a car which can, next to your home, be the place where you feel most safe. However, even then we need to remember that almost all 'car crime' happens when you are out of the car.

These statistics come from Home Office Bulletins, the British Crime Survey 1988 and the Commissioner of Metropolis Report 1989.

Notifiable Offences Recorded by the Police, England and Wales, 1989

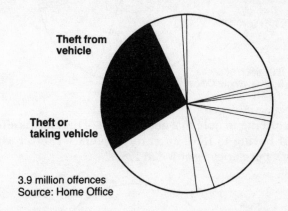

Theft from vehicle

Theft or taking vehicle

3.9 million offences
Source: Home Office

Car crime currently represents just over a quarter of all recorded crime.

Theft of property from a vehicle is matched only by criminal damage and in cases of criminal damage about 45% of offences* are against motor vehicles. When the theft of vehicles are added, then auto crime represents the highest category of crime.

In many of these cases the victim has presented the thief with the opportunity or inducement to carry out the crime by

*Source: Metropolitan Police.

either leaving property on open display or parking the vehicle in a secluded position so that the thief can work quietly.

The next most likely crime that we are likely to become victims of is that of burglary. A fifth of crime is burglary, though about half of this is not against the house but burglary of offices, factories etc.

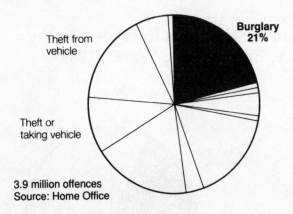

Burglary 21%

Theft from vehicle

Theft or taking vehicle

3.9 million offences
Source: Home Office

It is disturbing to note that about a fifth of burglary is effected without having to force an entry to premises. Over 440,000 domestic burglaries recorded in 1989.

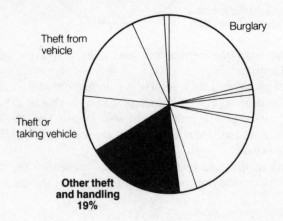

Burglary

Theft from vehicle

Theft or taking vehicle

Other theft and handling 19%

Simple theft is the next crime in descending order just under a fifth. This is the theft of unattended property, usually left on display by the victim, such as a hand bag over a chair in a restaurant or at the office or left on the shop counter: the wallet, money and cheque book left in an unattended jacket. House keys and even a name and address could be taken in this way.

Criminal damage accounts for 16%; 6% for theft from shops.

Violence against the person is about 5% of the whole.

Fraud and forgery at about 3%; robbery 1%, this includes all armed robberies on banks, building societies and security vans.

Coming an equal last of all recorded crimes is theft from the person at about 1%.

This is commonly known as mugging, forceful taking of property but *not* using violence against the person or threats to carry out the crime.

Finally sexual offences, total less than one in a hundred of all crimes. These are crimes which are so often perceived as far higher.

When we actually split the sexual offences into categories we find:

Sexual offences recorded by the police in England and Wales, 1989

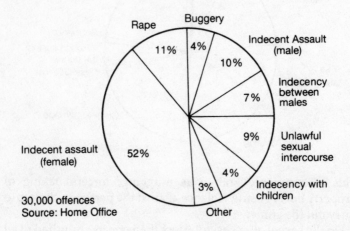

Rape 11%
Buggery 4%
Indecent Assault (male) 10%
Indecency between males 7%
Unlawful sexual intercourse 9%
Indecency with children 4%
Other 3%
Indecent assault (female) 52%

30,000 offences
Source: Home Office

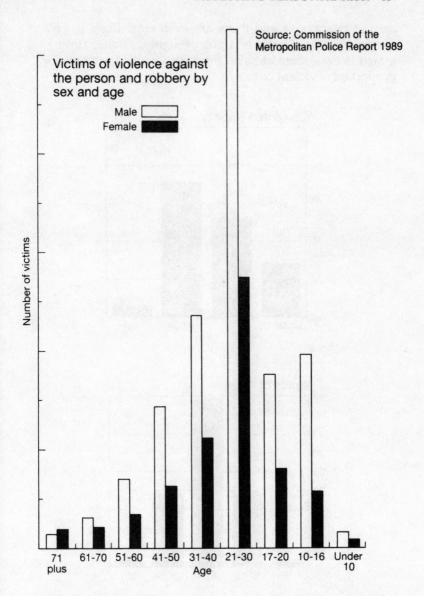

Source: Commission of the
Metropolitan Police Report 1989

Victims of violence against
the person and robbery by
sex and age

Male
Female

Number of victims

71
plus 61-70 51-60 41-50 31-40 21-30 17-20 10-16 Under
10

Age

These figures show that men are twice as likely to be an assault
victim as the women across all age groups. Men between the

ages of twenty-one and thirty are even more likely to be a victim. If in the vicinity of a pub or night club after closing, a man is even more at risk. Domestic assaults form a major proportion of violent crimes.

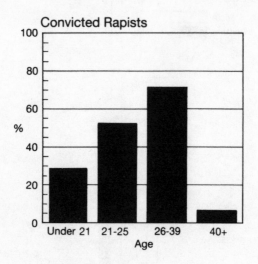

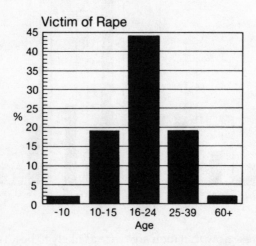

Getting these Statistics into Perspective

To make these stark figures more real John West shows that you are more likely to be a victim of the crime of robbery and theft to the person, which we would most commonly know as 'mugging', if:

- you are a man – less likely if you are a woman
- you are a woman aged between nineteen and thirty-five, or a man aged between sixteen and thirty – less likely if you are fifty-five or over
- you return home from work just after the rush hour, less vulnerable during peak times
- you travel regularly on London Underground between four pm and midnight
- you are out on the streets as a pedestrian regularly between the hours of eleven pm and midnight
- you carry a handbag
- you carry cash in your rear trouser pocket
- you visibly wear jewellery round the neck
- you are out in public on foot alone, less likely in groups of three or more
- you regularly take short cuts on foot via side-streets to reach your destination
- you prepare to resist and fight: you have a much better chance if you run away, scream or shout.

What about Sexual Crime?

The majority of rapes took place between people who knew each other and most happened in a building. You are more likely to be a victim between the ages of sixteen and twenty-four and least likely under ten or over sixty years old. The typical convicted rapist is between the ages of twenty-five and thirty.

If you look again at the categories of sexual offences that might also present you with a different perspective. When you really look at the facts, much of the indecency with children is committed by men with boys; the same is true about unlawful sexual intercourse and buggery. Add to this a percentage of the rape figure and it is not difficult to understand that the sexual offences against males almost equals those against females! It is also useful to note that it is arguably more acceptable for women to report such a crime.

The emotive fear of becoming a victim does not bear any resemblance to the actuality of crime itself. It makes a nonsense of society's endeavour to insist that women are the natural victims. I now feel ashamed, not that I worried and cared about my daughters, but rather that I expected my son just to be able to cope. It is perhaps time we looked at reality with more clarity.

Facing the Facts

Why should most of us get the picture so wrong? Perhaps it is because we have found it easier that way.

History
Most people feel comfortable with the notion of the male defender; after all, men are usually taller and certainly physically stronger.

One of the theories of aggression is that of *instinct*, aggression seen as necessary for the survival of the species because it ensures that the strongest will survive and overcrowding will be avoided. However, this kind of aggressive behaviour of the male is much more likely to have been acquired through life's experiences and the expectations of others. The 'macho' image, hyped up by the media and demanded from the male (not only by females but also by themselves and other males) reinforces this learning and the validity of this stance.

Without striving and dominance the human race could not have survived our struggle for existence. However most current thinking is that this is in fact due to an inherent capacity for self-assertion rather than aggression. Aggression is seen as the harmful result of directing self-assertiveness against another person.

True assertion includes respect for others. We can all probably benefit from reawakening our use of this skill. We will be discussing this under the chapter entitled Communication.

Society today

The frustration/aggression theory can (in anthropological terms) be seen as one of the major explanations of violence in our society today. Frustration considers both external events and opposing internal conflicts. Studies have shown that an animal which is frustrated can react by violently attacking the offending objective. The male can still be seen as the natural 'breadwinner' but many cannot get a job. He may be the one to thump the table when trying to make a point, desperate to maintain his status and self-respect. Others kick out at life in more disastrous ways, such as violence at football matches or demonstrations. A more mild example is the frustrated driver drumming his fingers on the car door when held up in a traffic jam.

The displacement theory of aggression makes sense here too. The man who has been 'passed over' for a job, been made redundant or damaged his car may take this aggression out on others. In this model, aggression is passed on from boss to husband, husband to wife, to child to the cat; or perhaps from manager to deputy manager, personal assistant to secretary, client to stranger. Many of us can recognize ourselves in this chain.

Aggression as a form of success

Although we use the noun aggression (and incidentally incorrectly) almost always as an expression of disapproval, we frequently use the adjective as a term of praise. 'Aggressive marketing', 'aggressive policies', 'aggressive pursuit' of news stories by reporters, the police 'aggressively' tracking down criminals are all acceptable in the business, political and establishment world.

We can learn as a child that a well-aimed thump can earn us a much envied toy from a submissive school mate. We model ourselves on our parents and peers. If our environment has established that aggression is the 'norm' we are likely to imitate that behaviour.

This theory that we learnt to be aggressive can explain some truly violent behaviour. With certain respected elements of our culture, television, videos, pop stars and current heroes, such as those in the field of sport, seemingly whipping up or condoning aggressive behaviour, it is hardly surprising that individuals can turn to violence.

Culture
It is not aggression as such which is frowned upon in our society but rather who it is that is being aggressive. We find it acceptable to call a man aggressive but to call a woman aggressive is definitely a 'put down'. Aggressive women are dubbed 'unladylike' or 'unfeminine'. We apply the same 'rule' to those we consider to be of 'low status'.

Men and women are different
Unfortunately as women have striven for equality of status and opportunity, they have neglected to build on their strengths and have misunderstood their really much-favoured position. Many women have believed in the myth of their vulnerability; they have endeavoured to ape male responses, roles and physical reactions to aggression. We have failed to realize that meeting aggression with aggression will most probably escalate into confrontation – and confrontation into violence. With confrontation both sides can get hurt and one side inevitably will!

Both men and women need help in learning how best to protect themselves. Men need to be encouraged to have the strength to avoid, defuse or deal with an incident rather than adopt an aggressive stance. Men also need relaxation techniques to release the rush of tension experienced when faced with aggression which can easily lead to the reflex action of, for instance, a clenched fist.

Women need to gain confidence in their own abilities and to

behave assertively when appropriate instead of behaving submissively. They also need to learn relaxation techniques. Pro-
longed tension in a true trauma situation can result in their
usually helpful physiological responses being blocked by a total
'freeze up'. For instance a woman about to be raped can be
traumatized to such an extent that she can fail to operate,
behaving like an automoton – 'Do as I say, do as I say!' – and she
will obey. With the flow of blood restricted by her tension, the
essential hormones and oxygen will be less help; she will
actually be unable to think.

Action Plan

The management of aggression is not a gender issue but one of
concern to women. Though there are signs that aggression and
violence is increasing and it is fair to wonder at the amount of
under-reporting, looking back over this chapter, the facts are
still quite clear.

Very few of us, though too many, are likely to become a
statistic of true violence, aggression or sexual offence and the
majority of victims will be men.

However more women are afraid that they will become a
victim and most men are unaware that they could be at risk.

* Fear makes you feel and act as though you are vulnerable
* Lack of awareness can make you a more likely target

The other kinds of aggression suffered by both men and women
we will all meet, often quite frequently, in our daily lives. These
are verbal abuse, harassment, bullying, innuendo and silence.
These can be debilitating and emotive and should not be
ignored. However, all these forms of aggression rely on getting
a 'rise' reaction from you which will then make you an even
more likely victim.

In all cases tension and stress control are a vital element which
we need to learn to enable us to manage aggression in ourselves
as well as others. We can learn to use anxiety to our advantage –
so our next chapter gives you some ways to help yourselves.

....

Anxiety

....

Anxiety and fear can be very disabling when you are
faced with aggression and violence.

Reducing stress and controlling tension can enable
us to use fear to our own advantage. Learning the
skills of relaxation is an invaluable aid to personal
safety.

This chapter will:-
- widen your knowledge and understanding of stress
  and tension and also its application to aggression and
  violence
- teach you some practical techniques to enable you to
  practise releasing tension in moments of anxiety.

The chapter will cover:-
- the definition of stress and tension
- the functions and advantages of fear
- the physical/psychological effects – fight/flight
- the relevance of this to the work, home, trauma
  situation
- the threat of over-stress
- how tension control/relaxation techniques can help
  control reactions and enable you to control yourself
  and manage aggression.

At the end of this chapter you should be able to:-
- recognize tension in yourself and how it affects your
  own performance
- understand how your anxiety affects other people
- perform and put into practice the 'Quick-Action Ten-

sion Release', to enable an avoidance response to aggression without any escalation
- consider the possibility of overstress
- know ways to combat stress, aid sleep and cope with your own aggression
- find some ways to combat long term stress with solutions.

Fear of what might happen makes you anxious. This anxiety can make you feel and appear vulnerable or it can have the opposite effect of winding you up so that you can act aggressively yourself without thought. Both reactions are more likely to result in you actually becoming a victim.

The understanding of stress and tension is fundamental to you being able to manage aggression. The practice of tension control techniques and relaxation will help you assess, re-assess and deal with problems. This is particularly essential when facing a potential, actual or imagined dangerous situation. It is vital when you need to respond effectively to real aggression and violence.

Think of your response when walking home through a dark street. You suddenly become aware that someone might be following you; your expression freezes, your ears almost feel they are stretching backwards as you locate the sounds, 'How near are they? Are they menacing?'

You cross the road and it might be that the grunting jogger just ploughs on! But suppose he crosses over too, you cross over again. He follows you. You might feel angry and turn to face the oncomer or more likely run away out of the suspected danger; you might feel 'rooted to the spot'; frozen until you feel secure again.

Let's consider another situation. This time you are at work. Your immediate manager is very impressed with an idea you have had which will not only save money for the department but also make it more efficient. The manager recognizes that this is the chance to make his mark at a regional meeting, which he is soon to attend. You know that if it is well-received you will get not only a pat on the back but possibly a rise too.

You work long and hard on this project. The manager has laid great stress that the project will never succeed unless you make sure it looks cost-effective. The day before the meeting arrives, you work late into the evening, you have a friend who uses desktop publishing and together you make sure it really looks good. The next morning, exhausted but pleased with your work, you hand it over to your impatient manager. He flicks through, 'good' he says, 'well done' – but he turns to the end and says, 'Where are the statistics?' And then, you remember, you have left them at home – ready, waiting but not here. The manager needs them '*now*'. The tension increases, you open your mouth and not a sound comes out. The manager snaps again, 'Well, come on I'm late already,' – all that you can manage is a high-pitched squeak!

Anyone who has tried to have an argument with someone who does not answer back will realize how frustrating that can be. Without any response the situation escalates, panic sets in as both the manager and yourself see the possibility of a valuable opportunity slipping away. In hindsight you could have said, 'I'll fetch it and send it up by Fax,' but by the time you recover your wits, the manager has left in a huff.

On that occasion the situation was developing between colleagues but of course it can be a customer who sets up the problem. Think of the person who always calls into the post office just before closing time. They stand there at the back of the longest queue, crossing their arms in mock condemnation, nodding sympathetically to fellow patient people standing in other lines! 'It's always like this in here – very badly organized. They haven't a clue.' Discontent spreads insidiously.

The clerk recognizes the customer and sighs, catching the eye of the person beside her. 'Why me?' she thinks. 'I was going home on time for once.' The customer gradually comes nearer, so does the querulous voice. The clerk clenches her jaw and feels her eyes twitch. 'I'm taught to smile, I must be polite, I've got to relax,' she says to herself as the tension increases. She does smile, she is polite, but as she leaves her desk she slams the drawer shut, snaps the hatch down, bangs her hat on her head and is sharp with a person who stops quite reasonably to ask the way. Later that evening her family ask if she is feeling alright. She has in fact got a splitting headache.

Anxiety and Performance

Anxiety and fear can also help us react well. However, as you can see from the curve in the diagram, too much and it is then that you lose control of the situation.

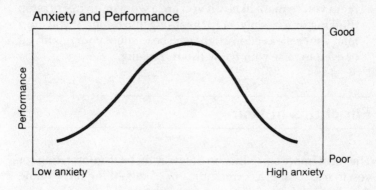

Anxiety and Performance

The Advantages of Fear

Fear is natural, fear is not a weakness; many of us feel frightened or nervous at different times. You can use fear as a safety mechanism; it is a natural danger signal. When you acknowledge this, it can be a source of strength.

If you listen to your feelings you are much more likely to

keep control of a situation instead of losing it. Let's use fear to our own advantage.

Let Your Fear Guide You

Most of us think of fear as a negative instinct or emotion but, if you look at it positively, it's a strength.
* Fear is an early warning signal telling you that something is wrong and to get out now!
* Your fear is a more reliable warning than waiting to look for anxiety in other people.
* Acting on these feelings means taking control. If you ignore them you're more likely, if you are a woman, to freeze, stop thinking or, possibly, stop breathing altogether. If you are a man your reflex action might well be to shoot your mouth off or even to raise your fist without thinking.

Functions of Fear

The most important function of fear is that it is information for you to use. Fear is a better indicator of something threatening than looking for signs of anxiety in others.

It signals the possibility of danger. Stop and assess. It is far better to know what is making you feel frightened than to let those feelings build further.

It can be a natural reaction when you are dealing with change or the unknown.

It reminds you that your fears may have come from frightening situations in the past. Do not ignore them. They have a realistic base.

When adrenalin floods the system it makes the hair stand on end. This is very obvious in an animal, but as humans have little body hair there is little visible effect. However, with a shock our short hairs stand on end and we feel the reaction as a creeping sensation on the skin, especially on the back of the neck.

Although this may not signal anything to anyone else, it is a sure sign to yourself that you are in an 'alert' situation. Your instinct is giving you a clear warning that something is wrong. Do not hesitate to take action to minimize the danger.

Reactions of the Body to Fear

The body has other ways of giving us signals that we are nervous and afraid, some time before it registers in our conscious minds. We must recognize our own particular physical responses to fear so that we can respond quickly.

These may include:

Stomach tightening	Cold hands and feet
Stomach churning	Sweaty palms, forehead, top lip
Hunched shoulders	Jaw tightening
Rigid spine	Wobbly legs
Breath holding	Heart beating fast

If you hold your fear inside or pretend it does not exist you ignore a situation which may become very threatening indeed. If you delay action you may become paralysed; you may stop moving, thinking or even breathing. Let your body tremble; any form of action helps to bring out strength and is better than freezing up. It is vital not to hold your breath, a regular supply of oxygen to the brain helps you think clearly and keeps the vocal chords open in case you need to shout.

Fear and Anxiety can Affect Others

While we can use fear to our own advantage we also need to very quickly take control of our physical reactions so that we can reassure those around us. These vibes of our feelings and thoughts about others and their effect on us can be very powerful.

The Quick Action Tension Release, which is described below, will enable you to operate at your best both physically and mentally in nearly all situations. The Olympic runner who is overstressed cannot run well and may pull a muscle; the TV performer who is over-nervous cannot think or perform at their best. If you constantly practise the Tension Release exercises they will become almost automatic. This will allow you to put all your energies into dealing with your life and its stresses as they come along.

Preventing the 'Black Out' – When Tension moves into Trauma

When the 'Red Alert' becomes 'Black Out' you will be either unable to move, speak or operate coherently or you might lash out thoughtlessly. Either way you may put yourself in jeopardy. To prevent this happening, teach yourself to be aware of your 'fear' warnings, and recognize your increase in tension so you can immediately put into practice the Quick Action Response to Tension.

Quick Action Response to Tension

Rules

Don't say to yourself, 'I *must* relax – you are likely to tighten up still further.

Practice is essential, it does not come naturally!

Begin to get 'in touch' with your body; as soon as you feel tension of any kind, tense up still further and then release completely.

Remember it is worth it, this technique really does work.

General practice (sitting in a chair)
Clench your hand into a fist until you feel your fingernails digging into your palm and you can see the whiteness of your knuckles.
Release – completely, including your arm, shoulders, jaw and neck.
Stretch your fingers along your thighs until they rise at the tips.
Release, completely, as above.
Push your shoulders downwards.
Release.
Push down your back, into the chair.
Push your heels into the floor.
Release.
Expel all your breath in a sigh and relax so that your lungs will fill with air.
Do the routine again so you can feel it but so that it is almost unseen to those around you.
This can be progressed to standing, facing another person talking to someone else; talking to someone, shouting.

Constant Stress can Become a Threat to Personal Safety

What is stress? When I was a Director/Founder of a health related organization, we took a survey of many people of all ages, in all walks of life and following many different occupations. The results were fascinating. We asked each person to write down all the activities of his or her day, hour by hour, indicating those found enjoyable, relaxing, pleasant, routine, unpleasant, challenging or stressful. Everyone had a totally different idea of what was understood by stress.

Some charts were so full that, when we had read to the end, we were almost gasping. They were peppered with 'S' for stress, together with many 'challenging moments' and 'enjoyable times'. These people were living life to the full, and when we met them, gave the impression of being vital and happy without overstress. Other charts were boring and with hardly any change in occupation or feeling day after day. Sometimes these were marked with only 'routine' or 'pleasant' hour after hour. You could see from these charts that there were no ups and downs, no excitements, no challenges and, when you met them, these people were often tired and depressed.

We all need a certain amount of stress in our lives if we are to feel fulfilled, vital and active. As one doctor put it, 'Stress is a demand upon our energy and without it we should become bored, remain emotionally immature and there would be no progress in human endeavour.'

Certainly, the right proportion of demands upon our energy will keep us looking younger and living longer. However, if we have more stresses than our own particular make-up is able to withstand then we will break down. Either physically or mentally, we will cry for help.

It is a question of balance. But you need to do your own weighing up, setting your own weaknesses against your strengths. Your ability to withstand overstress will also change within yourself from time to time. Everyone is very much under pressure from our life events. This covers any change in your life, either good or bad, such as marriage, children, job, home, promotion, redundancy, illness or bereavement even Christmas and holidays.

'Overstress' is the word we coined to describe the overloading of an individual stress capacity. When your stress causes constant tension, then you are 'overstressed'. With each person this stress level will be different. What is stressful for one person is not necessarily so for another, and emotional stresses cannot easily be compared between one person and another, nor can they be compared in the same person in succeeding years. Everyone needs to be regularly taking stock and assessing their own balance sheet.

Stress Personalities

Studies have shown that people with personality characteristics referred to as 'Type A' have a higher level of adrenalin and noradrenalin circulating in their bloodstream. This leads to an increased deposit of fats in the blood vessels. The problem is that living on a permanently high state of alert (such as the hard driving, hostile, critical and demanding Type A) can get to be 'intoxicating' and self-perpetuating, leading to more damage. People in high-stress jobs find it difficult to change to more mundane ones. They almost have to withdraw off the adrenalin much as drug addicts have to experience discomfort when 'kicking the habit'.

Recognizing Stress

One of the first steps to take is to try and recognize your own stress. We all have our own stress level so it can hinder you if you try to compare notes with anyone else. Stress can be divided into three sorts.

* First, of course, there is 'Obvious' stress such as we all feel when having to make a public speech, or go for an interview.
* Then there is 'Hidden' or 'Unconscious' stress. For example the feeling of annoyance you may repress about your parents, children or spouse. This type of stress can go on unrecognized for some time.
* Finally there is 'Unnoticed' stress. This can be unconsciously experienced say during travel (a driver on a motorway can have a pulse rate over 100 beats per minute for several hours).

These three types of stress can occur in all settings; the family, work and even in our social life. The symptoms of stress vary from person to person. You can have such symptoms as

anxiety, depression, nightmares, poor concentration, irritability. You can also have physical complaints such as a
general lack of energy and fatigue, headaches, backaches,
palpitations, abdominal cramps, loss of appetite, insomnia
etc. You need to recognize your own 'stress signals'.

Changing Behaviour

As well as physical signs of stress you can change your pattern
of behaviour when you begin to find your stress/tension level
too much to bear. An overstressed individual may disregard
tasks even if they have a high priority; they may also block out
or disregard new information; they may become detached
from situations; have sleep disturbance; a 'don't care' attitude;
they may develop a 'defensive' front; may fall behind with
reading and correspondence; lose interest and energy; become
easily tired and feel a drop in personal motivation.

If you notice these symptoms in a previously highly-
motivated dynamic person (the most vulnerable people are
often perfectionists) or if you begin to recognize them in
yourself, it is important to help yourself step back from the
situation. Continuing on can lead to what is termed 'burn out'
which will probably need medical help.

The 'Constant' Tension Response

But what happens if you are unable to respond with any
'action' when your body is fully prepared and ready? – there
you are lying beneath the bed clothes convinced there is a
burglar downstairs, your heart beats, your blood pressure
rises, you grow pale, your pupils dilate, you breathe faster,
feel butterflies in your stomach and your mouth is dry; you

start to tremble and want to go to the 'loo', but you dare not move.

Similarly day after day the boss or committee might thwart some plans which you have painstakingly worked out and considered and because of your less-advanced position you have to accept their decision, clench your fists, grit your teeth and go back to the drawing board again.

Likewise, quarrelling, anxiety, decisions, deadlines, and of course many more occasions and feelings, leave you with your responses 'pent up' and with no outlet. Your tension reactions have most likely set in motion all the 'Red Alert' responses but because the appropriate response in each case isn't to run and burn off the reaction you are left instead with all the added chemicals flooding your body.

Everyone has an individual pattern of physiological and psychological response to an 'alert'. This pattern will tend to be repeated when another signal comes.

This means that one person may show a marked increase in heartbeat each time while sweating only very little, another may perspire profusely; one person might show a rise in blood pressure, another an increase in gastric acid, or perhaps severe muscle tension. We develop and increasingly develop our own particular physical reactions to these calls on our energies.

This results in our developing our own physical warning signals when tension has reached an uncontrollable level. You might recognize one or some of these physiological symptoms:-

- throbbing head or headache
- grinding teeth, impacted nerve
- twitching eyes, tremulous voice
- pain spreading up the neck over the back of the head
- tightness in the throat, a feeling of choking
- aches between the shoulder blades
- nail-biting, damaged cuticles, twiddling thumbs
- palpitations and chest discomfort
- skin rashes

- vomiting and indigestion
- diarrhoea and/or frequency of urination
- backache in general, especially in the lower back
- tiredness, weakness, sweating, trembling, breathlessness, fainting or insomnia

Our psychological symptoms can include:-

- increase in smoking
- increase in alcohol intake
- a marked increase or decrease in appetite
- inability or constant desire and ability to sleep
- feelings of tiredness and exhaustion
- absent-mindedness, inefficiency, loss of interest, lack of concentration
- loss of sex drive
- feelings of inability to cope
- irritability, impulsiveness, loss of co-ordination, depression

All these can be a reaction to stress. Of course some of them may be symptoms of some other cause but if you have checked that you are not ill and you frequently experience one of these reactions you should take heed. They are your warning signals that excess tension is making your body suffer. They may be unpleasant but they are useful.

The Effect of Constant Tension on Aggressive Situations

We can all recognize the fact that when we are tired, distressed or worried we can act on a 'short fuse'. We are more likely to react to aggression with aggression, misread another's intentions or let fly at the innocent who just happens to be 'the final straw'.

Coping with Aggression within Yourself

When you are overstressed and confronted with aggression, it is easy to react in an aggressive way. You try to defend yourself, maintain status or 'get your own back'. The more defensive you become, the more tendency there is to focus on your own feelings and to regard the other person increasingly as a threat.

There is nothing shameful in a defensive response to hostility. It merely does nothing to help the aggressor out of his aggression, and it may make things worse for you. All of us experience a sense of personal frustration at times. We want something badly and circumstances deny it. We ask for a particular day off and are refused. It is part of living in human society that we feel a conflict between personal desires and external restraints and prohibitions. Being overstressed makes this worse.

The Development of Angry Situations

The most serious forms of violence are almost always preceded by strong feelings of anger. Angry situations develop through four stages:

* Trigger
* Interpretation
* Arousal
* Behaviour

Imagine a situation where your neighbour plays loud music late at night. You ask yourself – should I (1) discuss it with him over a cup of coffee, (2) play my own music even louder, or (3) bang on his door when this is going on and threaten him?

This is how the row over the noise could have developed.

Trigger – You have started a new demanding job and need to get up early.

Interpretation – The neighbour knows this and you think he is making a noise on purpose.

Arousal – You get really angry one night, your pulse races, you start to sweat and clench your fists.

Behaviour – You go up to his door and threaten to hit him or kick the door down.

Result – Major confrontation and violent behaviour.

If you lose your temper easily and that makes the situation worse you need to think about why this is and work out ways in which you could change your behaviour. Ask yourself a few questions:

What things wind you up?

How often do you lose your temper?

What happens when you lose your temper?

Do you take it out on:

- others, by shouting, being sarcastic or screaming at them
- yourself, by blaming yourself or feeling that you are 'no good'
- hitting cushions, pillows, digging the garden, shouting or singing in the bath

The last option is the most healthy in more ways than one!

Achieving Relaxation

Everyone benefits from learning relaxation techniques: Athletes need it to perfect their abilities, thinkers to increase their concentration, performers to release their energies and everyone to aid their self-protection.

Even normally relaxed people can benefit and should not neglect to practise this skill. They may well need to use it in times of emergencies and without the skill they will have nothing to fall back on, and they should examine what they think of as truly relaxed.

Exercise
Walk more often for a start! Walk everywhere you can; leave the car at home, forget the bus or at least go on to the next stop and enjoy some fresh air.

When you walk make sure your posture is good, your head is well balanced and your neck stretched; keep your eyes looking forward. Place the first foot on the ground in front and push onto it using the ball of the foot behind (this involves considerable ankle work), swing the arms gently. Practise this way of walking, it lessens the strain on the back and quickens the pace automatically.

Swimming is one of the very best sports to achieve not only a fully-exercised but also a relaxed body. However to do most good it is important to swim well and regularly. Swimming has the highest rating of all activities in improving suppleness, stamina and strength, it also stretches the body as well as supporting it so that there is no undue strain on any limbs or joints.

Other sports which can help are badminton, squash, basketball, jogging or running but it is essential to mobilize and warm the body first. Too many tense people rush straight into exercise. This can do far more harm than good. Over-thirty-five-year-olds might consider having a fitness assessment before embarking on a strenuous sport.

Diverting your 'mind'
Music can be a superb soother and tranquillizer, it can also release inhibitions and raise the spirits – it is even better if you move because movement is almost a necessity for draining off the chemicals aroused by the tension, so dancing and singing can be very therapeutic. Playing an instrument too is excellent and conductors have a job which holds the record for the highest lifespan.

Learning something new, reading, writing all can be helpful. So can a change of environment, holidays, visits, being at home or going out to work, all these may help.

Massage is one of the most ancient forms of natural healing.

Meditation using a form of chant, to focus the mind until a trance-like state is achieved, lowers the blood pressure dramatically. There are several different techniques and they need to be learned and mastered.

Sleep is essential to your well-being. Without it you can become tense and nervous and when you are anxious and stressed you can suffer from insomnia. It can become a vicious circle. Sleep not only refreshes the body it also, through dreams, restores the mind and discharges tension.

So if you are looking for a good night's sleep yet you find yourself tossing and turning, and wide awake though tired, what steps can you take to help yourself clear your 'racing mind'? First of all recognize that your mental activity may well have triggered off a 'Red Alert' response. In that case it will be beneficial for you to get up and move – to the bathroom or to the kitchen – and then when you have cooled and calmed down, go back to bed and make yourself comfortable.

Then quite deliberately:

- visualize a room or place where you feel safe and at home
- look around slowly and see the objects and the features (or people) if you have placed them there
- look around again faster this time
- repeat for a third time
- choose one point (an object, person or point) and keep your eyes fixed and try to think your way around
- do not let your eyes move (go back to the beginning if they do) but now repeat the thinking around again.
- You will fall asleep (if you do not cheat)!

A few more ideas? Animals can help: dogs are companions, stroking a cat's fur can bring down the blood pressure. Gardening can be most satisfying. Sex too can play its part. As a doctor in Hong Kong told the colony's Financial Women's Association 'sex is a good antidote to stress and tension' but he added 'the only problem is its inaccessibility in certain situations such as a traffic jam!' Tension Control Techniques might prove more useful.

Boredom

If boredom is your stress – keep some challenge in your life. Journey by train rather than join in the rush-hour traffic. Variety at work will help too.

Twenty Tips on How to Live with Stress

- Work off stress – physical activity is a marvellous outlet
- talk to someone you can truly trust
- learn to accept what you cannot change
- avoid self-medication, such as alcohol, nicotine, too much coffee, tranquillizers etc
- get enough sleep and rest
- take time out to play
- do something for others
- take one thing at a time
- agree with someone – 'Life is not a constant battle'
- manage your time better
- plan ahead
- if you are ill don't carry on as if you are not!
- take up a hobby
- remember that the answer lies with *you!*
- eat sensibly and exercise regularly
- don't put off relaxing – practise our techniques
- don't be afraid to say 'no'

- know when you are tired and do something about it
- delegate responsibility
- be realistic about perfection.

Long-term Relaxation

Memorizing a 'technique' sounds difficult but in fact as you gradually become familiar with the moves and routine of TCT (Tension Control Techniques) the body will begin to respond automatically and eventually you will find yourself putting the technique into operation when needed without conscious thought. However, this eventual result does not just happen. It takes some concentration, time and thought to master the skill. For a skill it is: relaxation is not for most of us a natural habit, so it has to be learned. But it is worth the effort. To make it easy we will take it step by step:

- the first week you should concentrate on reading and 'doing' the technique
- you should then progress to thinking and recognizing tension and release
- by then you should be able to remember and feel the tension release
- next you should practise continually and consciously apply the tension release during 'stress moments'
- TCT should become almost automatic
- you can then also try the sleep exercises, deep meditation/relaxation, and massage as well.

The Tension Control Technique works on the premise that only a fully contracted muscle will fully relax when it is released; and that as tight muscles signal to the brain that there is an 'alert' to be responded to, relaxed muscles have the opposite effect. It is a simple straightforward idea; the beauty of it is that it works! To release any tension you have in your body, work steadily from the top to the toes, clenching the groups of muscles tightly, holding them and then releasing completely. Give yourself time to really feel the tension and then savour the relaxation with each move.

Before you start you will need to make sure you are in a position to be able to relax without any effort. You should be able to breathe easily (no constricting clothes or slumped position) and have time for uninterrupted concentration. Allow yourself at least ten minutes, if possible completely alone.

Prop your book open on a table at a distance you can comfortably read. Find a chair with an upright back in which you can sit easily, facing the book; your back and shoulders should be supported, your knees slightly apart slightly rolled outwards, and your feet flat on the ground. If you have short legs put your feet on a stool or otherwise raise them so that you can completely release the tension in your legs. Let your arms hang loosely with your hands on your lap. Now read through and follow the instructions slowly. Remember to keep breathing easily and regularly throughout.

Start at the forehead. Wrinkle up the skin and frown between the eyebrows . . . hold it . . . let it go and release. Now frown hard, involve the whole scalp, feel the tightness . . . hold hard . . . release completely, feel the tension in the scalp relax.

Now for the eyes. Screw them up just slightly, feel the wrinkles at the sides . . . hold it . . . let go and release. Screw them up more tightly until there is only a pinprick of light . . . hold . . . and release. Screw them up tightly until the nose and forehead are involved . . . hold hard . . . let go completely.

On to the mouth. Pull sideways slightly . . . feel the tension . . . release. Pull the mouth into a smile . . . hold it . . . let go and release completely. Draw the mouth into a grimace . . . hold it hard . . . let go and relax.

Now for the jaw. Clench the teeth together . . . now release. Clench the teeth and jaw very tightly . . . feel the tension . . .

release completely so that the jaw drops, the mouth opens and the tongue falls back.

Next the shoulders. Lift slightly, hold . . . now drop. Raise the shoulders higher . . . hold them . . . release and let them fall back. Lift the shoulders to the ears . . . hold hard, let them go and feel the tension release.

On to the hands. Clench the hands into a fist and feel your fingernails in the palm . . . hold . . . and release. Clench the hands hard until the knuckles show white and you feel the tension in the shoulders . . . hold hard . . . let go and feel the tension release.

Now your trunk. Push the small of your back into the chair and feel the abdomen tighten and your pelvis move . . . hold . . . release . . . Repeat, making the movement stronger . . . hold longer . . . let go completely and feel yourself sink into the chair.

Down to your feet. Push your heels into the ground, feel the tension in the calves and thighs . . . hold . . . let go. Press down hard . . . hold tight . . . release completely.

Continue to sit for a moment, concentrating on breathing in and expanding, holding the breath briefly and then expelling as a release.

When you have mastered the commands and responses, it might help to lie down in warmth and comfort (a pillow under your neck and knees if you wish) and at the start:

- Lift your head and look at your toes . . . feel the tension and release . . . repeat
- start at the toes and tighten your calves, buttocks, hands, shoulders, face, hold and release . . . repeat
- now close your eyes and think of nothing but yourself while you go through the routine slowly and steadily.

As you become more practised you will begin to be aware whenever your muscles are under tension, and you will naturally tense and release them. There will be times when you need to take the actions deliberately, and that is when you will be really amazed at the results – such as a clear mind, quicker thought and the ability to master tricky situations without producing aggression on either side.

Preventing Problems

Strategies to avoid aggression and becoming a victim of violence are always the first choice before attempting heroics. Assessing, reassessing and reacting to instinct play an essential part in helping you to be aware of dangerous points in your daily life. Anticipating and recognizing a risk, then taking action is a practical formula for you at home, out and about, on public transport or at work.

This chapter will:
- teach you some practical ways to be safer when out and about
- enable you to assess the risks you could easily deal with in your immediate environment
- consider your safety at work and suggest that employers and employees should work together to reduce risks.

This chapter will cover:
- anticipation and prevention – aware and alert
- instinct and intuition
- ensuring you are not an easy target
- increasing personal confidence
- action plan – practical steps to a safer life
- being travelwise
- out and about safety plan
- in the car
- on your bike
- public transport – bus, train and underground
- preventing problems in your house

- obscene phone calls
- safety at work
- looking for a job
- lone business-woman travelling

By the end of this chapter you will be able to:
- be confident enough to listen to your instincts and act on them
- be able to take responsible actions when travelling by yourself or on public transport
- be aware of your surroundings and what represents a risk
- know your responsibilities as an employee and equally those which your employer carries
- understand why employers and employees have a dual role.

Having realized that your chances of becoming a victim of aggression and violence are very low you would also look at ways you can actually reduce those chances. By turning your fear and anxiety to your advantage – you can prevent the risk.

Of course the following ideas are only suggestions. You can choose to ignore some or even all of them but at least you will have a chance to make an 'informed choice'.

In getting on with our daily lives, this often means travelling on our own or being out late at night. It would be good to feel that we could go about our business when and how we choose, free from abuse. However, though the statistics show that most of us are unlikely to become a victim, we also have to face the fact that none of us is invincible.

Many people say to me, 'Why can't I live my life as I like? Why should I take special care walking down a road or not be able to wear whatever I like?' I agree, provided we do no harm to others, we should be free to act as we wish but I would suggest that doing this from a sound basis of knowledge rather than ignorance gives you a better chance of living a fuller, happier and safer life.

Far too many incidents are followed by the victim saying 'I thought it would never happen to me,' 'I imagined I was streetwise,' 'I felt this sort of thing only happened to other people.' It's easy to be wise after the event.

The trouble is that it is difficult to fully realize what it is like to become a victim unless you have really experienced it. Being mugged is painful, not only physically but also mentally; having a burglary is much more than losing your worldly goods, you can feel almost as though you have been raped – dirty, lacking in confidence and trust in others. Having trouble when you travel can inhibit your working and social life; being abused or harassed in the workplace can sap your self-esteem.

Humans are not like the cartoon characters or those card-board soap opera survivors. Humans have feelings, people bleed, we get hurt. We can exercise free will and in doing so we can choose to do much to protect ourselves.

One of my jobs is to teach swimming to people who are afraid of water. They may have nearly drowned, or are elderly or physically disabled. My aim is not only to teach them to swim but also to swim safely wherever they are. I teach my students to automatically look round the pool, study the beach, approach lakes and especially rivers with caution. They learn to be aware of the possible dangers, assess the means available to save others or themselves and reassess the practicalities of putting them into practice. Swimming is a great joy but it is potentially lethal. I hope none of my students are afraid of water when they have attended my classes but each and every one of them respect the element and their relationship with it.

This I believe should be our attitude to our own personal safety. If we take reasonable precautions we can enjoy our freedom. Of course we cannot entirely escape evil but very few of us will have the mischance to be that unlucky.

Anticipation and prevention are the principles of self-protection – the way to avoid confrontation. Assessing, reassessing and reacting to instinct play an essential part in avoiding danger.

Awareness is the key. Don't be frightened into taking ridiculous steps in the name of self-protection. A few precautions such as letting people know where you are, avoiding potentially risky situations, carrying a personal alarm in your hand when you go home at night, will help you to be safer and to feel safer, which is important because confidence is vital.

Consciously build up in yourself knowledge of your own strength and power. You are likely to be much stronger and faster than you realize. Most people never test themselves to find out what they can really do. Part of self-preservation is having a good idea of your physical capabilities. Being fit is a big help.

Alertness. Stand up tall, keep your feet slightly apart for good balance, keep your head up and your mind focused on your surroundings. If you look like someone who knows what is going on around you, you look less vulnerable.

Research shows that the typical 'muggable' person walking along does not move their arms in rhythm with their legs and plonks their feet down on the pavement with a graceless thump unlike the swinging walk most people have. They give the impression of being physically unbalanced. Other observers of 'muggable' types have noticed that they tend to be in a daze or a daydream, to walk hunched over, and to pay no attention to their surroundings, often looking lost.

This description does not refer to people who are disabled. On the contrary, people with disabilities are often very much 'in touch' with their own bodies and extremely good at knowing their physical strengths and weaknesses.

Assess and reassess. Whenever you are out and about, at work or in your home, it is sensible to assess any situation, assess the safety and escape and then reassess what you feel you could or should do in an emergency. Do this consciously until it becomes an automatic reaction.

Do this in the workplace too. Travelling to and from work, choosing what work to do and who to work for, working with your colleagues and for your boss, going out of the office, working in your home and going to other people's, all should be consciously assessed, reassessed and then reassessed again. You should know what is expected of you by your employer, and how you yourself are able and prepared to behave. And if you feel uncomfortable with a person or in a place, if a warning signal goes off somewhere deep inside you, if you feel scared or even just uneasy, do not ignore it. Act upon it straight away.

Remember your instinct. Instinct and intuition are valuable indicators (whatever experts tell us they are really based on). Recognize them for the source of strength and power which they are.

There are many times when people say, after being in a threatening situation, 'I knew there was something wrong, but I thought I was imagining it,' or 'I told myself not to be stupid.'

Strictly speaking instinct is not a 'sense', like taste, hearing, sight, smell and touch. Our instinct comes from our natural learning. We perceive a great deal more than we are aware of and this comes to our aid when one or more of our five senses alert us to potential problems.

Intuition is easy to ignore. It's hard to define; society places greater confidence on reason and logic. Intuition becomes something almost mystical and therefore not to be trusted. If we have been taught not to put ourselves first to meet other people's needs before our own, to be 'polite', we may learn to mistrust our own gut responses and give other people the benefit of the doubt.

This intuitive sense is a key to avoiding potentially aggressive situations. Our sensitivity to our intuition is heightened when we have relaxed any tension and are alert to our surroundings and our own reactions. Be in touch with your senses and your own particular responses, and have the confidence to trust them. It may not be obvious why, yet the feeling that something is wrong is very powerful. When you are in tune with your feelings and reactions you are equipped to act promptly. With practice your actions will be instinctive or automatic.

Make sure you do not present yourself as an easy target. Know where you are going and look as if you want to get there. Look up your route beforehand if you need to negotiate any difficulties such as desolate areas or docklands, and make any necessary changes. Note the roads, and keep them and the address plus the telephone number easily to hand.

Wear shoes that are easy to walk in and ensure that you can run if necessary. Footwear should be secure and give you good balance.

Confident Body Language

* Walk tall; hold yourself straight, with your shoulders back. Slouching makes you look off-guard and unsure.
* Be alert, keep an eye on your surroundings, and make sure you look as if you know where you're going – even if you don't. Looking lost is an open invitation to an attacker.
* Keep your eyes peeled constantly, but don't look around nervously; concentrate on where you're going. Never shuffle along with your eyes on the ground!
* Keep your arms relaxed, swing them gently as you walk. Don't tense up or wring your hands.
* Look calm and serious. Avoid eye contact with strangers.
* Stand straight. If you're waiting for someone, a bus or train, stand with your weight evenly distributed on both feet – you'll look confident and ready for anything. Don't hop from foot to foot, lean on one leg or twist one leg around the other.
* When travelling on buses or trains sit up straight, with your hands in your lap, so you'll feel and therefore look more confident. Don't nail-bite or fiddle with your bag or case.

To Help You Feel More Confident

* Hold your keys in your hands as you walk along, with the appropriate key ready so you won't have to fumble as you

reach your door and you can let yourself in quickly. Ideally have a key light so you can see the lock, if it is dark.

* If you are really concerned about the area into which you are going, carry a shriek alarm, make sure it is a gas one as these do not run out without warning. Also ensure that it fits easily into your hand, it will be of no use whatsoever in your bag or briefcase! It is important to realize why you are carrying such an alarm and how it can help you.

* In my experience it is very rare for the public to rush to your aid if you let one off. Most of us hearing a burglar alarm on a house or car are likely to pass by wishing someone would turn it off! We do the same with personal alarms. However the actual shriek is earpiercing and if you are prepared to bring it up sharply by an attacker's ear they will end up clutching their head in pain. This gives you the vital time to get away. Do not stop to think, move.

Out and About: being travelwise

The Trust published the results of its first research project in March 1989. This was entitled 'The Risks of Going to Work' and was carried out by the London School of Economics.

Many of the results surprised us but we were particularly interested in the fact that 'out-workers' – those who worked from or totally outside their office or home – were most at risk.

* 8% of people were found to be likely to suffer assault on their journey to or from work
* 1 in 5 reported having an unpleasant occurrence on their journey

These figures do not match the impression given by media stories. The research also showed that men are much more vulnerable to attack than women. You only have to look at the crime figures of the London Underground to understand the reality:-

* 75% of the attacks are men on men
* 85% of the personal theft is men from men

Travelling around does however present some real problems. We all want to live a free and active life and everyone has to undertake regular journeys of some kind. With some commonsense, forethought and informed judgement, many of the risks can be avoided. Getting around can then be the enjoyable adventure we ought to be able to expect.

Keep alert

When you travel on your own, by foot, bicycle, or car you are 'in charge' of yourself; the only one to blame if you make a mistake. Moreover if you are at all aware of personal safety you are likely to be alert to potential problems and alive to any hazards.

But on public transport you can fall into the trap of giving all that personal responsibility to others. On the bus, tube or train you often follow the advertisers' advice literally and relax completely, allowing the vehicle to 'take the strain'. But if you drop your guard and quash your instincts, situations can escalate before you realize they have even started.

The wise passenger never loses sight of the fact that public transport is still a public place. There is open access to stations. No-one is vetted, everyone is acceptable as a passenger. Moreover when we travel we are often unable to move away easily and avoid any trouble.

However, this responsibility for personal safety is not one-way. The operators have a duty in law to carry passengers safely from one place to another without harm. The companies realize that *feeling safe* is a vital element to achieve contented customers. Verbal abuse, graffiti, sexual and racial harassment as well as outright assault and attack are all unacceptable.

The companies need your business and want to promote a feeling of 'customer care' and a comfortable environment. To get this right, they and passengers need to work together. The company needs to inform the passengers of all the safety systems they install, and know when you are not satisfied or when an incident has occurred. Without this knowledge they may fail to act. The passengers need to take reasonable care to look after themselves and communicate any problems.

Don't hesitate – your action may well help many others!

The 'Travelwise' Safety Plan

Prepare yourself for the journey	Wear sensible clothing
	Know your route
	Know where alarms/escapes are
	Tell someone where you're going
Look confident	Sense of purpose
	Radiate non-vulnerability
	Watch your body language – stand tall, look aware and alert
	But carry an SLT alarm if you feel it is necessary
Avoid risk	Decline offers from strangers
	Keep to familiar territory
	No spur of moment choices
	Try not to use unlit cash machines
	Keep a hand free
Never assume	It won't happen to me
	It's only a short journey
	They look respectable

Remind yourself that your purpose is to Anticipate and Recognize any Risks and then take Action to Remove and Avoid them. If you do this you can begin to tackle any problem with increased confidence and without fear!

Here are some ideas of what you might consider when you create your own Travelwise Safety Plan.

Preparation
* If you have to carry things, try to use a bag that will go over your shoulder. Use a small one slung across your body under a jacket or coat, or a shoulder bag with a short, strong

strap and good fastenings. Make sure it sits close to your body with the fastenings innermost.

* If really necessary be prepared to give something up such as your bag. This means that you should be careful not to carry your whole important world wherever you go. Filofaxes and their like have a lot to answer for. They can become so precious that their owners cling to the bag containing these reams of information at the expense of their own safety.

* Do not wear a scarf with ends hanging down the neck. If possible, tuck the scarf out of sight, so it cannot be used to attack you.

* For the sake of your ease of mind and those you care about, leave behind in an accessible place all the details you think would be needed by the police if anything unfortunate did happen.

* Familiarize yourself with your routes and surroundings. This will make it easier for you to avoid danger spots and to know where you might be able to seek help if you ever need it. Get to know where there are concealed entrances, where the lighting is bad and where there are pubs or garages or public phones which might be useful should you think you are being followed.

* Be prepared to walk a long way round if necessary. It is a temptation to let laziness or haste cloud your judgement. It is not worth taking the risk.

* Keep enough money on you for a cab home if necessary. Use black taxis or other licensed cabs, or a minicab firm known locally for its good reputation.

* If you work in a secluded or undesirable area, organize a lift-share system with friends or colleagues. Ensure they wait until you have safely entered your home.

* Attackers do not like noise and when their stealth is compromized by a yell from you they may well beat a hasty retreat. A deep loud shout is very effective; breathe out with a sigh which will relax your muscles, breathe in, drop your jaw and expel the air into a forceful noise.

* Be prepared to bang on doors and keep yelling even if you only suspect you are in danger. If you feel apprehensive do

not enter the house unless more than one person opens the door. Know where public phones are. Carry a phone card as many phones now accept these. Remember the police are always available via 999.

* If you get no response, shout an instruction such as 'Phone the police' – people are likely to react when given something to do. In extreme situations a heavy object such as a stone thrown through a window will invariably bring instant investigation.
* Be especially careful when leaving a bank; do not window shop on your own at night; be extra vigilant on Fridays or pay days. Avoid getting into routines when collecting or delivering money.
* Make sure you have some change on you, enough for public transport or a parking meter.

Look confident
* If you must carry a bag, do not hold it too tightly to your body. This could indicate that it contains some things of value.
* Remember that alcohol affects your judgement of both people and situations. Know your limits.
* Walk purposefully at a good pace and keep to well-lit busy streets. Do not allow yourself to be distracted; avoid eating, drinking or reading while you walk. Do not wear stereo headphones, they cut out street noises.
* Keep your awareness alarm in your hand when you walk home at night. Be prepared to use it. An attack alarm brought up sharply by the assailant's ear and pressed against it is incredibly painful.

Avoid risk
* Try to keep both hands free. Avoid carrying heavy bags in both hands at the same time. Whenever possible carry nothing. Don't walk with both hands thrust into your pockets.
* Place essential valuables such as wallets in an inside pocket secured with a safety pin. This is an infallible way to stop a pickpocket. Alternatively use a body belt or 'bum' bag.

* Use caution in conversation with, or being overheard by, strangers. Avoid giving your name, address or place of employment, or revealing you live alone.
* At all times of day avoid deserted places, dark buildings, bushes, waste ground, car parks and alleyways, especially when you are walking on your own. Allow space round parked cars; be wary of cars with engines running and people sitting in them.
* Vary your daily travel routine – avoid a very regular pattern of movements.
* Be on guard in crowds and try to go round them, especially if they are juveniles. Be wary of people jostling you or becoming an obstacle, particularly at bus stops, getting on or off trains and queueing in shops.
* Try not to pass through a subway on your own; take advantage of other people who are passing the same way to act as your escort.
* If the street is deserted, walk down the middle of the pavement, face the oncoming traffic to avoid kerb crawlers and remain alert to your immediate surroundings. If you need to pass through a 'risk area' occupy your thoughts by actively thinking about what you would do if faced by a problem. Look for escape routes and be prepared to take action if necessary. If the pavement is narrow walk on the kerbside to avoid being grabbed by someone in a doorway.
* At night, unless it is absolutely essential, do not use a pocket torch – this will show up your presence and make it more difficult for you to see a potential assailant. It is better to let your eyes become accustomed to the dark. It is useful, however, to carry a torch so that you can check your car before getting into it.
* If you do think that you are being followed, trust your instincts and take action. As confidently as you can, cross over the road, turning as you do so, in order to see whoever is behind you. If he crosses too, be prepared to recross again and again. Keep moving. If he continues to follow, make for a busy area – a pub, service station or other public premises, go in and phone the police and a

friend. Also tell the publican, cashier or anyone else who is
likely to help you.
* If a vehicle pulls up suddenly alongside you, turn and walk
in the other direction – you can turn much faster than a car.

Never assume that it cannot happen to you!
As we saw in Chapter 1 your chance of actually being attacked
is very low indeed. However, you can reduce this still
further if you can avoid particularly vulnerable situations.
* It is folly to hitch-hike however desperate you are. All of us
are open to attack – play safe.
* Never be tempted to accept a lift with a stranger even if you
are wet, tired or very late. The driver may claim to be a taxi or
minicab – anyone who reads the news will remember that
taking chances like this can have disastrous consequences.
* Beware of a stranger who warns you of the danger of
walking alone and then offers to accompany you. This is a
ploy some attackers have been known to use. Ignore
requests for directions, cigarettes or a light at night.
* If you jog to work you may have some advantages. You will
be wearing ideal clothing to get away from someone quickly
and you may be fitter than your pursuer – but do not bank on
it.
* If you ring for a mini-cab in a pub, disco, etc., make sure
you're not overheard. Someone might pretend to be the car
you ordered.

The Social Round

* If you are going to a party or staying out late, plan your
journey home in advance.
* Arrange for someone to meet you or travel home with a friend
you can trust. Keep a cab number and your fare handy.
* Judgement of people and situations can be affected by too
much alcohol – so be sensible.

* Don't walk home with, or accept a lift from anyone you are unsure about, even if you know them.
* Make a pact with a friend should either of you be stranded, the friend could send a cab or come and collect you.

Cabs

In London, hackney carriages (Black Taxis) are licensed by the police. However in London mini-cabs or private hire vehicles are unlicensed. Most mini-cab drivers are reliable and honest, but like all professions, they have their bad apples. During 1990/1991 the Trust commissioned some research into the relative risks of taxi and mini-cab use. This was undertaken by Dr John Groeger and jointly financed by the Woolwich Building Society and the Department of Transport. The survey was the largest of its kind ever carried out in the United Kingdom.

Two thirds of the sample were drawn from London where there is little regulation of mini-cab services; the remainder were from Manchester which has a comparable balance of taxis and mini-cabs by largely similar regulation of both services.

Substantial numbers of incidents were reported in both London and Manchester with London mini-cabs particularly being associated with unpleasant experiences. It is my view that we rapidly need a change in the law. Meanwhile, please follow these guidelines:

* Make sure you have the phone number of a reputable cab company. Ask your friends for a recommendation.
* When you book your cab you must do so by phone. Ask the company for the driver's name and even his call sign. Ask what type of car he has.
* If you are calling from a public place, try to avoid doing so where someone overhears you giving your name etc. Anyone could pull up and call 'cab for Mary Smith' so when your cab arrives, check the driver's name and confirm his company.
* If you can, share a cab with a friend, so much the better, it's cheaper too. Make sure you both get out at the same destination if possible.

* Whilst you may not wish to appear unfriendly, always sit in the back.
* If you do chat with the driver don't give any personal details away.
* If you feel uneasy with the driver ask him to stop at a busy familiar place and get out.
* Before you arrive at your destination, have your cash ready, leave the cab and pay the driver.
* Have your door keys ready and enter your home quickly.

Beware of bogus mini-cabs

Some people do not work for mini-cab firms at all. They put an aerial on the roof of their car and have a pretend handset. They unlawfully ply for hire at busy night-spots. They gain fares by calling out 'Someone ordered a cab?'

On a busy night with a shortage of transport – it could be tempting – DON'T, it could be dangerous.

Travelling in your own car

Apart from the physical security aspects of auto crime you must consider yourself as a target in a vehicle. You're safer in some ways – more vulnerable in others. Sometimes you'll find yourself a long way from home in unfamiliar surroundings.

* Stay in the car as much as possible. Keep the doors locked. Think about keeping the windows closed.
* Keep any bags out of sight. With a window open, it's easy pickings for a snatch thief when you stop at the lights.
* Keep your car in good working order and carry extra petrol in a special safety-approved portable petrol can. Consider an automatic latex puncture aerosol to get you to the nearest garage.
* Always keep a map handy so you won't need to stop and ask directions.
* Make sure you have change and a phone card for a pay-phone in case of an emergency.

Parking the car
* When leaving the car always lock valuables in the boot.
* Lock your car even when you are on a garage forecourt and go to pay for petrol.
* At night, park in a well-lit place. And when you get back, remember to check the back seat before getting in. Have a good pocket torch handy and the keys ready in your hand for a quick getaway.
* If you park in daylight, consider what the area will look like in the dark.

Incidents which might happen to you in a car
* If you see an incident or accident or someone tries to flag you down, *don't* immediately conclude you should stop to investigate. Think first – is it genuine? Could you help? It might be safer and more practical to report what you have seen at the next convenient telephone or police station.
* If you think you're being followed, try to alert other drivers by flashing your lights and sounding your horn. Or keep driving until you come to a busy place, a police, fire or ambulance station, pub or garage forecourt.
* If you own a car you *should* be a member of one of the breakdown organizations.
* Whilst expensive, if you travel a lot, you should get a car phone. Ask your employer for one.
* When stopped at traffic lights or road junctions, avoid eye contact when a car pulls alongside and particularly if the driver sounds its horn or occupants leer at you. Like obscene phone calls, if they don't succeed in annoying you, they have failed.
* If a car travels alongside you constantly at the same speed, immediately slow down and let them pass. Drive to a busy place – garage forecourt, a police station or hospital etc. If you have a car phone, lift it up to your ear as though you were phoning the police. Consider buying an imitation car phone for these eventualities.
* If a car (which is not a police car!) pulls up in front of you and causes you to stop. *Never turn off the engine*. You may flood it

if you try to restart. Stay calm and when the driver leaves his car and almost reaches yours try to reverse as far as possible whilst continually sounding the horn and activating your hazard lights, whatever time of night. As long as your doors are all locked and your windows are closed you are fairly safe.

* If someone tries to force a partially open window down, be ready to retaliate with anything innocent to hand. A de-icer spray, a fire extinguisher, can be very effective.
* If they get their hand through, consider your car cigarette lighter. Hit the intruder's hand with your shoe, especially a stiletto heel.

Motorways

Travel on motorways is becoming an increasing concern, especially when a breakdown occurs or assistance is needed. Opinions are divided as to what you should or should not do. For instance there is a debate on whether you should remain in a car and put up a HELP sign in the back window or walk to the telephone, and having made the call, stay in the car or stand on the bank.

* First of all if you can safely drive to an emergency telephone then do so, stopping with the front passenger door of the car level with the telephone as far to the left as possible.
* Switch on your hazard lights. If leaving the vehicle do so by the nearside door. Leave any animals in the car.
* Never cross the carriageway to reach a closer telephone. Never reverse your car to a telephone.
* If you cannot drive further, a marker post (every 100 meters) will point to the nearest phone; they are set 1,000 meters apart. You will never need to walk further than 500 meters.
* No money is required. As soon as you lift the handset, it will start ringing in the police control room. You do not need to say where you are, they will know.

* Stand behind the phone, facing oncoming traffic, so you can see if anyone approaches you. The passing traffic makes it very noisy. You may have to shout.
* Tell the control if you are a woman on your own. They will alert a police car to check you are alright. On some urban motorways they may even be able to see you on closed circuit television.
* If your car is not near to the phone then note the numbers on the nearest marker post. Tell the control room the problem, having your breakdown organization card ready and your registration number.
* The highway code section 173 advises *you* to decide whether or not to stay in the car or leave it and stand on the verge. It is a fact though that ten per cent of all fatal motorway accidents take place by a vehicle colliding with a stationary car parked on the hard shoulder. In 1988, twenty-five fatal accidents occurred in this way.

When the breakdown truck arrives, check that he knows your name and has in fact been sent to you. Some breakdowns cruise waiting to pirate custom.

Crime prevention advantages must be weighed against remaining in a vehicle in a potentially hostile environment.

The Department of Transport, Police, RAC and AA's advice is to stay on the bank only re-entering the car if you feel in danger. Try to decide by taking all the factors into consideration, the weather (fog, rain, snow, sunshine) the time of day and whether it is a dark deserted country stretch or a busy urban well-lit area.

If you are travelling alone

Following a series of experiments Suffolk police tested the 'Help, Call Police' signs and now positively support them. However, they also say 'If you are broken down and display a sign, remain close to your car, in the passenger seat, if you decide to stay in the vehicle. Do not accept a lift or leave the area as this could instigate a major search when you or your car cannot be found.'

Whatever, if you are alone there are two options. You can either:

* If you decide to stay in the car remember the dangers of an accident happening. Keep all doors locked and windows closed.
* If you stand on the bank, try to stay out of sight of passing cars.
* Lock all the car doors except the passenger door which you should leave fully open so that you can get back in quickly if you decide to. Then lock the passenger door behind you.
* Do not leave the keys in the car.
* If you are by the phone and someone stops, use the phone to tell the police, give them the registration number of the car that has stopped.

On your Bike

Travelling by bicycle can be one of the safer ways to go. You are totally independent but because you are exposed to vehicles and the elements, it seems dangerous. Threats to the cyclist are not just those of physical assault. There are crashes, dogs getting in the way, the risk of breaking down in lonely places.

Keep your bike in good working order. Running repairs are better done at home than on the road.

* Pedal safely but speedily. Appear to have a sense of purpose.
* Give clear hand signals and respect the other traffic on the road; don't offend drivers.
* Look competent; wear the correct gear; reflector band, toe clips, helmet. Have the correct accessories such as lights in good working order. Mirrors can be helpful.
* If you are short-sighted, wear glasses/lenses. Spot trouble ahead, rather than riding into it.
* A piercing loud horn is great in emergencies. Have a screamer or a loud whistle on you.

* Carry an item of clothing to use in the event of wet weather and one for the cold.
* Carry a lock and key so that you can leave the bike secure if you breakdown and take public transport or a taxi if necessary, rather than having to stay with your bike or walk it home.
* Don't be afraid to pedal hard out of or around potential trouble. Your bike is really your ally.

Public Transport

Taking the bus
More people travel by bus than by any other means of public transport.

Now that the bus companies have been privatized, passengers may have problems with operators who may be tempted to see the safety aspect of their business as a threat to quick profits. On the other hand reputable companies have realized that a clean, comfortable environment not only encourages more passengers but also is the basis for greater safety. Some companies have also invested in modern design forms especially suitable for the elderly and disabled. Principles of good practice are laid down by the Department of Transport and enforced by the Bus and Coach Council to which ninety-five per cent of operators belong.

Taking care of yourself
* When waiting for a bus at night, try to stand in a well-lit place near groups of people. Walk on from isolated bus stops if necessary.
* When you get on the vehicle, try to sit near the driver and choose an aisle seat. On a double decker, the lower deck is the safer environment.
* If you find yourself alone on public transport with someone who you sense might harass you, try making yourself look as repulsive as possible. You could try picking your nose,

cleaning your ears, scratching or muttering to yourself; your inhibitions are less important than your safety!
* If you are molested or harassed in a bus, make a fuss straight away: the driver can alert the police or the head office if they have a radio. He can also keep the doors closed.
* When getting off a bus at night attach yourself to groups of people and walk purposefully to your destination.
* Know where you are going and which stop you need. Occasionally buses are suddenly terminated before the stop where you expect to get out. Do carry extra money on your person (not your bag) to avoid being stranded.

Travelling by train
British Rail have many unmodernized stations and old rolling stock. They are updating all stations, some of which have been described as badly designed, isolated, dangerous and unpredictable. BR have recognized that a clean environment is not only welcoming but also discourages crime. They are treating passenger safety as a priority and making improvements.

Taking care of yourself
* Try to avoid travelling in single compartment trains with no access to guards. There are still a few of these left.
* If you ever feel uneasy or are left alone or with one person in a carriage, do not hesitate – move.
* Pull the alarm quickly if you are actively intimidated or have been a victim of or seen an attack.
* Try to avoid travelling on the days of an important football match (unless of course you are attending). It is impossible to ban fans on service trains. The British Transport Police are empowered to confiscate drink brought onto the train and alcohol is also banned at that time from the trains and station premises.
* If you are in or see a potentially escalating situation go and search for or get a message to a British Rail official. They will come and assess the position and do their best to defuse the aggravation.

* If the incident merits it, the conductor will radio the driver. The train will then stop at the special phones along the line so that the driver can contact the police ahead at the next scheduled stop.
* If you know you are going to get off at a badly-lit, unmanned station at night, arrange for a taxi to meet you or a friend to pick you up.

Using the underground

With its enclosed and empty corridors and our natural fears of being underground, the tube can seem an inhospitable place. The atmosphere itself sometimes generates fear. Although the actual risks of becoming a victim are small our perceptions are much greater. Therefore London Underground launched a major strategic initiative in 1986 and this is gradually working.

Taking care of yourself
* Wait for the train in a well-lit place near groups of people and stand well back by the wall.
* When you get onto the Underground, try to choose the carriage which will stop near the exit opening at your destination.
* If you feel at all uncomfortable with your fellow passengers, move carriages at the next station. Don't just sit there!
* If you find yourself being molested, do not hesitate to make a fuss straight away. For instance grab the hand which seems to be straying when you are packed like a sardine in a tube during rush hour. Quickly pull it up above your head and say loudly: 'Who belongs to this?' You may be surprised at the result. It is vital to act quickly.
* Ask the driver to contact the operations or control room if you need help quickly.
* If you are attacked on a tube, shout for someone to operate the Emergency alarm so you can receive help more quickly when you reach the next station. Run through the interconnecting doors if possible.

* London Underground is standardizing alarms on trains. Until this programme is completed you will see both the push button and the pull down handle types in an emergency. Familiarize yourself with the position of the alarms on entering the train. Follow the simple directions given on the handle or next to the button.
* When getting off trains try to attach yourself to people leaving the station. Deserted stations provide opportunities for thieves and other criminals. If no one is there, walk briskly and purposefully. All stations now have public telephones – use them to call home.
* If you have seen an incident, seek staff assistance or look to see if there is a 'Help Point' and call for help. Station staff are always available in the ticket hall.
* Use the confidential Freephone Crime Line (0800 252525) to report any incidents to the British Transport Police.

Preventing Problems in your House

It is estimated that the average house burglary takes about five minutes to commit. This includes the time to spot the target, make sure it is unoccupied, get in, find the goods, get out and get away. A car theft will take even less!

If there are no signs to help, the burglar is already being made to take more time than they would prefer. If this time factor can be increased, and at the same time the criminal can be made to make a lot of noise and be conspicuous, they must start to wonder whether or not the crime is actually worth the effort! Our aim needs to be to make the burglar:-

– *Take more time* to commit the crime
– *Make more noise* to commit the crime
– *Look more conspicuous* while committing the crime.

Removing hiding places

It is clear that the areas most vulnerable to a criminal are those where he can work unobserved. *Remove any cover* that allows the criminal to be *more conspicuous*.

Consider *improving lighting*.
Consider *trimming hedges* down, thin them out
Consider trimming the branches of trees below the level of windows
Consider *removing anything* which would make it harder to see any criminal.

Making a noise

* Ask your local Crime Prevention Officer for a free home security survey – this will give you many ideas.
* Keep a radio playing when you are out.
* Some councils and charities provide security devices free of charge to the housebound and elderly. Ask your local Citizen's Advice Bureau.

Playing for time

If you have a caller you do not know – these are the police recommendations:
* Fit a door chain and spyhole. Installing outside lighting lets you identify callers.
* Before opening the door, keep the door chain on and ask for proof of identity. Keep them waiting until you're satisfied, even if it's a woman or child.
* All public service employees carry identity cards and are required to show them. Examine these carefully as fake ones can be used. The cards should include a photograph of the holder and the name of the organization. Don't be taken in by someone who says he's left his card behind.
* If you're at all suspicious about anyone, call the police at once by dialling 999. Don't worry if it turns out to be a false alarm.
* If you're selling your home, try not to show people around on your own. Tell your estate agent always to send a representative with prospective buyers. If this is impossible, make sure

the agent has made an appointment, verified bona fides and has given a name.

Personal precautions

* Give a key to a neighbour to hold.
* Never leave keys under doormats.
* If you lose your keys or move into a new home, have your locks changed.
* Never give your keys to workmen or tradesmen. Copies are easily made.
* When you are watching TV or having a bath lock the back door.
* Before you leave home lock all outside doors and windows.
* Draw your curtains at night to deter any Peeping Toms or other snoopers.
* If you have a shed keep it locked and make sure there are no tools around which could be used to break into your home.
* Always have the phone numbers of neighbours to hand so that you can contact someone quickly.
* Consider a phone that holds a 'memory' of phone numbers that dials the number automatically after pressing one or two buttons.
* Programme in the numbers of the public utilities, your neighbours, the local police etc.
* If you hear someone break into the house – don't confront the burglar. Try to escape by another exit, or retreat to a safe room and call the police. Then if you can, alert your neighbour, phone up, bang on the wall or in an emergency throw a heavy object through the window.

When you go away

* Cancel papers and milk, don't leave empty bottles out.
* Make sure your letter box is big enough to take circulars and 'freebie' papers.
* Ask a neighbour to keep an eye on things.
* Complete an 'Unattended House' form at your local police station.

* Fit a heat-sensitive light system which will light up any area when someone enters the zone.
* If you think there are or have been intruders when you return do not investigate. Contact the police immediately.

Design and planning

If you have a choice about where to live, you will be safer in a neighbourhood which has:
* short, direct and well-lit footpaths and walkways
* pedestrian routes that are overlooked by buildings
* well-lit, overlooked parking areas
* housing, where the people directly own the land surrounding the house or flat where they live. Highrise blocks surrounded by open parkland allow strangers to roam at will without anyone taking any notice.

Less safe are neighbourhoods which have:

* subways
* sharp bends which restrict views where there are long paths and walkways
* high walls and shrubs which obstruct clear views
* walls and shrubs close to walkways that could hide an assailant.

Don't just sit on any problems or ideas you may have for improvements. Take a pro-active stance and pass on ideas to your local Neighbourhood Watch or Crime Prevention Panel. Co-ordinated action is much more likely to achieve a response from your Local Authority. In my view better lighting, graffiti removal, more telephones and entry systems all need to be seen as high-priority matters.

Obscene Phone Calls

Obscene and indecent phone calls are a criminal offence. They are also very threatening and unpleasant. A one-off call, however, may have little chance of detection. Persistent callers may be able to be detected. The investigation of such crimes is a matter for the police who are assisted by British Telecom. Before it reaches that stage though there is much you can do. BT now have a helpline number and also issue leaflets. The police are now treating this very distressing offence in a more positive way.

Remember

The telephone is for your convenience, use it on your own terms and do not feel you have to talk to anyone unless you want to. If you are being troubled by nuisance calls make sure that a caller identifies himself.

If someone asks 'what number is this?' simply ask what number they are calling and then say whether they are right or wrong. It is not advisable to give out your name and address on the telephone unless the caller is known to you.

What can you do?
* As soon as you realize that you are receiving a nuisance or obscene telephone call, hang up, gently, showing no emotion. Many such callers hope for an emotional reaction and long conversations, as they would like nothing better than an exchange of insults. Do not give the caller the satisfaction; simply hang up. This advice is now accepted virtually worldwide.
* Some callers do remain silent just to hear what your reaction will be – it will not be much fun for this caller if you just hang up and let him listen to a dead line.
* If nuisance calls, especially silent calls, persist despite hanging up immediately, it is possible that the caller is known to you. Most random callers are put off if they do not get the desired reaction. If this is your problem now is the time to ask help from the police. It is a recordable offence and should be reported to the police.

At Work

Safety at work is an important area that we should not overlook. Whilst many people feel 'threatened' when travelling or when out after dark, we give less thought to our safety at work. Travelling can be part of work and certainly many people have to make visits to strangers outside their workplace.

It is however the workplace itself, coupled with the type of job, that can be one of the most risky areas. Either from the risk of assault because of the nature of the goods held on the premises, such as banks, building societies or an off licence late at night, or from the nature of work – DSS unemployment office, pub, school, housing office and many others.

In my role as Director of The Suzy Lamplugh Trust I have for some time been a member of the Health and Safety Executive Committee on Violence. That committee has gradually increased its standing and breadth of membership. At last I believe we are beginning to get the message across to employers that looking after the personal safety of their staff is cost-effective.

Jobs with higher risk
The HSE breaks down the types of interaction that can leave staff more at risk from violence as follows:

* giving a service
* caring
* education
* money transactions
* delivery/collection
* controlling
* inspecting.

Not only may there be a risk in relation to your type of job but also your safety in the workplace in general. Office and workplace thefts of personal property have always been a problem and unfortunately probably always will be. These type of crimes are distasteful and promote suspicion between colleagues which can in its turn cause tension and distress.

This section is not about interpersonal relationships, we will discuss that later. Here we can look at the practical steps you can take by yourself or with your colleagues which are designed to prevent problems and reduce the risks of aggression and violence.

Safety in the office
If you start work in a building early or leave late at night you should always appreciate that unauthorized people may enter the building unless access control is in place.

If the premises are wide open then this is an invitation to all and sundry to enter. An electric door lock to the front door of your building or even your department should be considered. A receptionist who controls access to the building is a good form of access control but consideration should be given to their safety too and thought should be given to the period before and after the receptionists are on duty.

Personal property
To leave your personal property on display is an invitation to the opportunist office thief. This is either a member of staff or someone who has wandered in off the street.

* Lock away your handbag or briefcase.
* Don't leave your wallet or money in your jacket pocket if it is left on the hanger, or over your chair back.
* Don't give your home telephone number or address to clients. If clients need to contact you after hours consider a mobile phone or pager.
* Don't get into a lift with anyone who makes you feel uneasy. Get out if someone enters who you feel uneasy about. Stand by the alarm button.
* Never go to an appointment without checking back that the client is genuine.
* When you leave the office, record details of your expected movements and the time you are due back and who you are with.

* If you change your plans phone in and report.

Office property/tradespeople/contract cleaners and security people

* Have a procedure for tradespeople calling at the office. Always check credentials.
* Office machinery should never be handed over for 'repair' or 'service' without checking that the repair or service was requested.
* Make sure that the service personnel, window cleaners, phone repair people, typewriter mechanics who call unannounced are genuine.
* Whilst it would be good to be able to trust people, you do need to check that they are genuine and not con men/ women.
* If an unknown face appears in your office, pleasantly ask if you can help or ask who they are looking for.
* If you slightly suspect anyone, then report them to security or follow your company procedure. Do you have a company procedure?
* If you found someone in your workplace whom you suspected or did not know, what procedure do you have, who would you report them to?

Violence in the work place

What is violence?
The Health and Safety Executive's working definition of violence is:

'Any incident in which an employee is abused, threatened or assaulted by a member of the public in circumstances arising out of the course of his or her employment.' The Trust would include colleagues and employers too.

Verbal abuse and threats are the most common types of incident. Physical attacks are comparatively rare in most occupations.

Is it my concern?
Both employer and employees have an interest in reducing

violence at work. For employers, violence can lead to low morale and a poor image for the organization, making it difficult to recruit and retain staff. It can also mean extra costs, with absenteeism, higher insurance premiums and compensation payments. For employees, violence can cause pain, suffering and even disability. Physical attacks are obviously dangerous but serious or persistent verbal abuse or threats can also damage employees' health through anxiety or stress.

All employers have a legal duty under Section 2(1) of the Health and Safety at Work Act 1974 to ensure, so far as is reasonably practicable, the health, safety and welfare at work of their employees. This duty can extend to protecting employees from assaults.

The Health and Safety Executive recommend an action plan. The best way to tackle violence is for employers and employees to work together to decide what to do. Special regard should also be paid to preventing problems, for example efficiency of glass shields for employees working with money, positioning of interview desks in vulnerable employments such as housing or hospitals, alarms, buttons and lights (who maintains them, operates and reacts to them?) and any other relevant points which are often recognized but also neglected.

There are a lot of cheap, even cost-free, measures that can be taken to reduce violence at work. Most of them involve procedures and managing the work situation – not costly building changes. For example, can someone see any strangers coming into the building? Where are cars parked? Do people working on their own habitually sit or stand near a phone so that they can call for help? If people are working on their own (for example, in a shop), is there a list of nearby shops to call to get help? Think about contributing to the situation by the placing of furniture and visibility. What about the siting of tills and stock? Having talked about this subject with so many organizations I could go on and on but when it actually comes to making decisions every work-place is different and I say to them. 'It is your problem – not my problem. However my interest is your safety so I do advise you to listen to each other and do some clear thinking. Don't leave it to chance'.

Companies should also have thought about how they will react when a crime has been committed. Employees who have been victimized should have the opportunity to have someone with them – without any questions. They may well need extra help to clear up and get going again. In more serious cases the company should offer independent, professional help by a counsellor, clinical psychologist or psychiatrist. These arrangements need to be made *before* the offence occurs. Post-trauma syndrome is very real and debilitating.

Finding a Job

Remember some jobs carry with them special risks for both men and women. Assess whether you are equipped, able and prepared to cope. Choose a job to suit your personality.

* Avoid advertisements offering far too much money for very little work!
* Avoid escort agencies and such like which cannot really vet their clients.
* Carefully check jobs advertised in newsagents or in the papers, especially if they do not give an address or company name.
* Establish the credentials of a recruiting company.
* If finding a job through an agency, make sure it is reputable; that it checks out its clients, visits the premises and provides detailed job descriptions.
* Ensure that any interview takes place at an office of either the employer or the agency.
* If, for any reason, you are asked to go elsewhere, make sure that it is in a public place. Take along a friend who can wait at a safe distance. If at all dubious refuse to go to the interview.

* If the inteview has to take place outside working hours, ask a friend to collect you at a specified time and tell your interviewer.
* Always make sure that someone knows you are being interviewed, and at what time you expect to return.
* During the interview, steer the conversation away from personal subjects that have no relevance to the job.
* No matter how well the interview appears to be going, avoid continuing the discussion into the social scene, over dinner, drinks etc.
* Never accept a lift home from the interviewer. Arrange your own transport beforehand.
* If you are offered a job abroad be especially careful to check out the employer and the type of work you will be expected to do, as well as the provision of safe travel and suitable accommodation. Ensure that everyone knows your where-abouts and contact details.
* Ask prospective employers what procedures they have for protecting their staff.
* Make quite sure you fully understand why you are being employed.

Then ask yourself:
* Have you got the job because of your qualifications, your expertise, your potential, your personality, or your looks? Any reason may be perfectly valid, but it is important for you to be aware of it, so that you can decide whether you are equipped, able and prepared to cope with the risks attached.

Travelling Alone for Business-women

Apart from all the other matters of personal safety that you have learned about there are others in relation to the use of hotels by the single business-woman.

* When booking a hotel, ask for a room near to the lift or preferably on the ground floor.
* When booking in at reception, make sure that your allocated room is not mentioned out loud by the clerk, someone could overhear it. When you book in ask to be handed the keys in an envelope.
* If you are given a room at the end of a dimly-lit corridor ask to change.
* If you receive phone calls in your room make sure you don't give your room number away.
* When in the restaurant make sure the waiter does not repeat your room number out loud. Normally you should have a room card, show him that.
* Try to use a hotel you know or a chain, where optimum standards are set.
* Don't invite clients to a meeting in your room; avoid a meeting in their room unless others are present. Use one of the public rooms or meetings rooms.

Communication is a Two-Way Business

We communicate with others in many different ways. We use verbal and non-verbal language to pass messages to each other which reveal our thoughts, attitudes and feelings. Approach and appearance can unwittingly raise aggression in others as well as ourselves. Stereotyping, prejudices, lack of understanding can all affect our behaviour. Being aware of communication techniques can help you convey what you intend and can produce a desired response in others without rancour. Your voice can help you calm an aggressor or ward off an attack. The way you use your body language can change a confrontation into a conversation.

This chapter will:
- widen your knowledge of the messages we take in from people we meet and on which we make judgments about them
- make you aware that other people unconsciously take in many messages about you
- teach you to be aware of how different people can be
- help you develop verbal and non-verbal communication skills which can defuse, control, calm or deal with aggression
- discuss harassment which can be very distressing and aggressive.

This chapter will cover:
- verbal communication

- verbal triggers
- using verbal control
- using your voice in an attack situation
- body language
- first impressions
- receiving and giving non-verbal signals
- clothes
- facial expression
- eye contact
- body movements
- body contact
- orientation
- personal space
- mood
- role play
- social behaviour
- controlling your emotions
- laugh and the world laughs with you
- harassment – bullying
- sexual harassment
- racial harassment
- communication techniques
- what is assertiveness?
- why be assertive?
- what are your rights?
- reactions to assertiveness
- assertive body language
- communication with other people.

By the end of this chapter you should be able to:-
- be aware of how much your behaviour affects others
- realize the effect people have on you
- recognize that your norm is not necessarily the same as someone else's norm
- understand that aggression may be crossed purposes and wavelengths
- know how to control an aggressive or potentially dangerous situation

- learn how to deal with distressing harassment in its many forms
- be encouraged to develop communication techniques to help with difficult situations.

When we are with our fellow human beings we constantly communicate with them and they with us. We send out and receive both verbal and non-verbal signals and consciously or unconsciously interpret the messages. We can all too easily misinterpret or misjudge others and they in turn can fail to understand us.

Appearance, approach, voice and language can all unwittingly raise aggression in others as well as ourselves. Awareness of this problem can reduce your risks still further.

Verbal Communication

We listen to the rhythm and tonal notes of a person's voice before we take in what people actually say. We are startled by a bellow, taken aback by a shout and disconcerted by someone speaking loudly. Some people are however loudmouthed by nature, youngsters get used to making themselves heard, other people are deaf and cannot hear their own voice. We make judgements, they do the same about us.

Whether we like it or not we react to an authoritative command; dismiss a submissive simper; feel exhausted by chatter which we can barely keep pace with, irritated by the slow, quiet whisper which we cannot really hear. We can get impatient with others but have we learned to turn the tables on ourselves?

I am Welsh and my voice can go up at the end of a sentence. To me this is quite normal but I have had to realize that this can appear peevish to some ears. Going into a pub the other day I heard someone say, 'Here comes trouble,' and all we had heard was an Irish voice. By contrast I had someone to help me with a class for elderly visually handicapped swimmers. They had never met her and yet they said, 'Oh she sounds so kind.' What they heard was a soft Irish burr.

The police team who were looking for Suzy were based in Notting Hill. They were preparing for the Notting Hill Carnival (though I got the impression that they were perhaps getting ready for a riot a long time before the event!). I asked them if they had considered the rhythm and volume of the voice. They looked at me as though I was slightly mad. A group of West Indians can, I explained, sound so excited that you can think a fight is about to break out when in reality they are only discussing breakfast. It seems important to take this into account.

My son had a Chinese girlfriend. When she talked with her sister their voices were fast and high-pitched and I would think something had gone wrong. They were only discussing the sister's children and I was mishearing the tone of the conversation. We need to listen with the appreciation that our ears may not be in tune with the other person's real meaning.

Do some experiments yourself. Practise making simple requests of other people such as:

> 'Excuse me I need to get past.'
> 'Could you please tell me the time?'

Try using a calm voice, an unsure one, a really serious voice, and now try an authoritative one and note not only the difference of your tone, pitch and choice of words but also the reactions of those to whom you speak. Experiment until you are able to remain firm, clear and polite. Listen to yourself on a tape recorder too. It can be quite a shock but remember how much you may be affected by tension. When you are tense your voice rises and once again this can aggravate a situation.

Verbal triggers

We all have words, phrases or clichés which act on us like red rags to a bull. My own 'trigger' is when someone says to me, 'I hear what you say'; I immediately conclude that they have not listened to a word I have said and are just repeating a fatuous line given to them on a training course. This may or may not be unfair. Whichever way, I immediately feel angry and the unfortunate person remains diminished in my eyes.

As we do this exercise in our training courses I realize that each workplace and location has its own pet hates or particular phrases. Various remarks can be made with double meanings, such as:

'With respect' meaning, 'I am just about to be rude.'

'We'll take that on board' – 'That idea goes in the bin.'

'I pay your wages' – member of public to Council employees.

'I want to speak to the Manager' – 'You are a female so you must be the secretary.'

'Why don't you go back where you belong?' – 'You are taking my place/job.'

It goes on and on. Play this with your friends. Each write down ideas on a piece of paper and then share your thoughts. You will be surprised how many you will have in common.

Now think to yourself – how many times do I use such trigger words to others? Sometimes we do it knowingly, at other times you realize immediately the words have left your mouth. In all cases we need to be more aware.

There are times, both in the house and work situation, I have caught myself thinking – 'What's the betting they make that excuse/bring out that old chestnut/repeat that saying?' I can find myself literally willing them on – 'go on *use* it! Make me mad!' All the time you do this you can find yourself tensing up ready to pounce. I have to realize I probably do the same to others too. Verbal triggers to anger need to be watched. They can be the spark which sets off a conflagration.

Using verbal control

If you feel you are not in immediate physical danger you may decide to try using verbal control to defuse the situation.

It does take confidence, self-control and sometimes a genuine sense of humour to calm down a really angry person. It is however perfectly possible provided you are not faced with truly psychotic behaviour, a person high on drugs or inflamed by alcohol.

The first essential is to reach through the anger to some point of contact. It is vital to establish some link on which to build.

> 'Can I have your name please?'
> 'Your address?'
> 'Can I help you, my name is . . . '
> 'You obviously have a problem, I am here to help you.'

In a calm, low tone of voice, keep talking, searching for the person to become aware of you as an individual human being.

When they do speak take them seriously. Listen to what they have to say. Empathize with their feelings, sympathize with their problem. Reflect their messages to you back to them so that they can hear and understand better what they are trying to say. Many an angry person is a poor communicator trying to make themselves clear.

'You say you are complaining about the poll tax? I am sorry you feel like that. It can be difficult.' 'There are only two of you at home and both of you are not earning? It is difficult when you have not got a job. Have you been out of work long?' 'You have been trying to claim a refund but do not understand the form? They're not easy. I do sympathize.' 'Come and sit down and we will discuss it.'

Now you have reached the control stage. This is the time to make sure you do not appear threatening yourself – sit at the same height or slightly below, at forty-five degrees and remember to maintain real interest.

'This form is to help you claim your due. Let us take it step by step. We will see if we can find an answer.' Once the form has been introduced, you can establish an adult relationship and a calm atmosphere. You can eventually refer back to the original complaint.

'Do you feel happier now? Are there any other problems you would like to discuss?'

However if when facing the angry person, you fail to make contact as you try to reach that person through their anger and they seem to be quite out of control, displaying wholly inappropriate behaviour, it may well be wise to break off contact at least temporarily.

'Excuse me, I think you need to see the manager.' 'I will just fetch a form, please wait until I get back.'

This will hopefully interrrupt their flow and allow them space to cool down.

The same verbal defusing strategies can be very useful with really difficult telephone callers. If you are faced with a real slanging match, keep an elongated silence your end, allow the caller to rant on alone until they begin to blow out the storm, before they regain their breath, come in yourself.

'I do apologize the line suddenly went dead (someone cut us off) do you mind starting again at the beginning? You had a problem, perhaps you could give me your name . . . your address . . . ' etc. The second response usually loses much of its vehemence.

Using your voice to 'voice off' an attack

Many people say 'I'd use my voice.' But would you? You may think you will be able to, but when it comes to it you would probably react in the way we discussed in the chapter on Anxiety. With a dry mouth, tight muscles and restricted blood supply, your voice will either rise or disappear altogether. Your voice, however, *is* a very good asset; how do you retrieve it?

First of all discover how to open your mouth. This sounds pedantic but in fact many of us lift our upper jaw (especially in attempting to scream or shout) and this causes the whole skull to move, shutting off, eventually, your ability to use your vocal chords properly. If you feel for the joints on either side of your face on a level with your ear lobes and then allow your jaw to drop, you will have discovered how to open your mouth properly.

Now place your hands on your diaphragm, sigh deeply so you can feel your muscles contracting and hear the air expelling. Release and allow the vacuum to fill with fresh air. Do it once again and you will feel relaxed, your blood will be able to flow and the oxygen circulate. You will be able to think, to operate, to act. If you want to give a potential attacker a surprise, expel the air with a bellow or as though you are about to be sick. You will be surprized at the effect it has on people.

If you need to shout for help do not bother to yell 'Help' or 'Rape' – most people will not react and many will just hope someone is play-acting and that it will go away. Shout an order 'Ring 999', 'I need the police immediately' or whatever is appropriate. People are much more likely to do as they are told.

Practise this skill – it needs to come as naturally as possible. When you are practising try to be out of earshot if possible. Beware of 'crying wolf'.

Non-Verbal Communication

Body language

So far in this book we have been taking a practical look at the world around us. I hope you have been encouraged to make some personal decisions on the need to consider active measures towards your personal safety and management of aggression. We are now coming closer to home and looking at our own attitudes and behaviour.

Whether you like it or not someone's appearance and approach can unwittingly raise your hackles. Prejudices, lack of understanding, stereotyping, (i.e. the images we unthinkingly form of other people according to their class and culture) and the 'roles' people play can all affect your attitudes and feelings as well. Being aware of this fact and the realization of the way it affects others is very useful.

We 'read' other people by the way they look, behave, dress,

sound and even smell! We then put this information together with our previous experiences, our childhood and school upbringing; we weigh it against the judgment of others on TV, radio, in magazines and above all against the opinions of our friends. We then decide that we 'know' them and put them in the appropriate pigeonhole in our mind.

We do this all the time quite unconsciously and without effort, often on brief acquaintance. In fact you need to do this, as a 'shorthand' to enable you to know who surrounds you and how to react. However we can allow ourselves to take in the wrong messages and consequently give inappropriate responses, sometimes with confusing, even upsetting or actually potentially dangerous results.

We also need to understand that other people are 'reading' us too. In this section you will begin to realize how you can communicate the messages you really mean and convey to others the person you are and the attitudes you intend.

First impressions
From talking to people who teach interpersonal skills I have learned that we take in our impressions of others quickly but usually in a certain order. Ask a number of people what they first notice about someone else and they are likely to say, 'Their eyes' or, 'Their smile'. However these observations are a long way down the line.

It's much more likely that first you register their age, race and their gender. From a person's colour we can make snap judgments about someone's 'capabilities' for instance to do a certain job, to be sympathetic or hostile to an approach or question, which may or may not match up to the reality at all.

On the issue of gender so many women have told me as I travel the country giving talks and training courses, that they are faced with the demand, 'I want to speak to the boss, please fetch him!' when they are in fact the manager, so it is painfully obvious that people make irrational judgments about gender too. One of the more bizarre I read was about two women who were arrested for suspected soliciting when the police saw them visiting dilapidated buildings with different men. These

'prostitutes' were surveyors visiting the properties with building contractors and potential buyers. On the other hand meet a
male nurse and it will be quite likely that we assume the white
coat means they are the doctor.

We need to understand that not only do we make quick
decisions about people, others have the same reactions to us as
well. Our 'norm' is not necessarily the other person's 'norm'. It
is so easy to misinterpret each other.

Receiving and giving non-verbal signals

You send out and receive information about the people you
meet by a whole range of non-verbal communication. You get
an impression from their general appearance and from this
you may weigh up a number of opinions. Are they tidy or ill-
tempered? Are they formally or casually dressed? Are they
wearing badges that say something about their political
beliefs? Do they look well cared for?

An averted gaze and slumped posture betray submission
without a word spoken; folded arms and thrusting chin signal
hostility despite a smooth tongue; a silky leotard looks good in
the gym and an off-the-shoulder dress is chic at a party but
both say something quite different elsewhere; whilst flaunted
tattoos and medallions produce varied effects on people. We
need to consider when we might need to cover up, to play cool
and avoid misinterpretations. It may be your right to behave as
you please but can you afford to take no account of the
shortcomings of others?

Clothes

A bikini looks quite acceptable on any woman when she is
by a swimming pool or on the beach. However if she were
to appear dressed like that in the High Street she would be
giving out completely different messages. Taking this back
to rather more down-to-earth examples the Trust were
having an advertisement made by a very well-known PR
company. They had offered to do this free and the Trust was
very grateful. I was certainly overawed and never having
been in that scene before I was filled with curiosity. When I

first met our young male team dressed in their tight jeans, open-necked shirts, gold charms, with a metaphorical assurance of 'I am creative' written all over their hairless chests, I immediately jumped to the conclusion that these youngsters were just what the Trust needed. (In actuality they had a great deal to learn.) However if my bank manager or my solicitor had been dressed like that I would not have thought they were worth the money.

On one training course I met a social worker. She was complaining about the amount of aggression she was 'continually faced with these days'. She excelled in the knowledge of her job, but I could understand why she had difficulties. Dressed beautifully in designer clothes, with jewellery to match, she did not present an understanding 'mother-earth' image which I sometimes associate with the health worker type in the standard long skirt and low heels. Instead she looked as though she had no idea what it was like to live in tough circumstances, which can gradually grind down the joy of being alive.

It was not only that which caused her problems. A social worker carries a standard workbag, the very presence of which indicates 'Power'. That well dressed girl enters someone's vulnerable territory with the power to recommend to the doctor to 'give granny a potty', 'remove granny to a Home' or condemn a family to a life with an incontinent senile person who is already making them feel guilty and behave out of character just by her daily presence. The social worker's very appearance makes a situation which is confrontational before even a word has been spoken.

Uniforms can be a problem too. As with the man who for several years walked round a well-known hospital wearing a white coat and was taken by everyone as a qualified doctor. This goes back to our reaction to the male nurse. We expect police, transport officials, the military to all be dressed for the part. However, research has shown that we the public react with submission to only a certain amount of gold braid; too many 'rings round the sleeves' creates confrontation. Experimentation is endeavouring to get it just right. Many of the 'care' professions now wear no uniforms or where it is essential, only a very low-key form of standard dress.

We have unwritten rules, in regard to clothes, the boundaries of which are nevertheless fairly variable. The clothes we wear do reflect current fashions but our response to them is usually several years behind the times. Big corporate organizations clearly draw lines on expectation of 'dress'. As people progress up the hierarchy they are permitted to gradually change. I was amused to visit one large organization and note how many 'old school ties' from a well-known department store were being worn to indicate the arrival at or signal the wish to progress to a higher position. Many people not having their wish fulfilled will endeavour to move to another company. It is well worth managers making a conscious note of the people they wish to promote so they can catch them before they are on the wing.

Dressing for safety is therefore a complex issue. You are likely to set up aggression in others if you do not present yourself as people expect you to appear. People got quite annoyed with me for instance when I wore my ordinary bright clothes after my daughter disappeared. 'Why wasn't I in black?' they kept asking me. To me, at that time, I could not face the fact that she might be dead. We were not working on the same wavelength.

You also run a risk if you wear what might be considered to an on-looker 'suggestive clothing' when you are out and about, especially after dark. A woman's tight, revealing dress may be worn by her to advertise her loss of weight or show courage after being ditched by her boyfriend but she could be seen quite differently by someone on the prowl as she made her way home. A young man can look quite frightening with shaved head or dyed hair sticking up like cockscomb. He may simply be showing that he is one of the crowd. It is of course their choice, it is our choice how we dress but we need to remember when we do so the impact we have on others.

Facial expression
Facial expression teaches us a lot about each other too. You can

often understand what someone is feeling or thinking. Your eyes and mouth are probably the most expressive and indeed may give out contradictory messages.

You can demonstrate anxiety, fear or embarrassment although you say you are fine. Your facial expression is probably showing your true feelings. Remember that others may be watching you closely for your reaction to what they say.

How do you look? Sit down in front of a mirror and now practise your range of facial expressions. Consider how you look and what happens to your face when you are

Tense   Cross   Dismissive
        Friendly   Calm

Now imagine that you are looking out from that mirror at yourself. How would you feel and react?

Eye contact

We have 'rules' which govern eye contact. The speaker will often look away from the listener, but will establish direct eye contact from time to time to make sure that they are maintaining their attention.

Frequently when the speaker is concentrating on what they are saying eye contact can be minimal, but when they are getting ready to finish, more frequent eye contact can be a signal for the listener to respond or to start speaking themselves. If the speaker does not establish at least some eye contact they may be distressed and uncomfortable about what they are saying.

A listener tends to look at the speaker during the conversation and will look away when bored. It is very difficult to maintain a conversation when a listener does not look attentive. Even the most articulate and talkative people tend to dry up in the absence of any response.

When someone is talking you demonstrate clearly that you are listening by using appropriate eye contact. The important word here is 'appropriate'. If, for instance, you maintain continual eye contact it can be interpreted as threatening and may precipitate violence. You have probably heard people in potentially violent situations asking aggressively, 'What are you staring at?'

The appropriate use of eye contact is of vital importance for interaction, but you do occasionally find yourself in circumstances when eye contact feels uncomfortable. It may sometimes be easier to focus on a point just above the bridge of the nose. This gives the impression of eye contact but may be easier to maintain in difficult situations.

Your practice here can last for a day or even a week. Consciously watch other people as you make eye contact. How often do you catch another's eye as you talk with them. How do they react to you? Do people show humour, embarrassment, shyness? At what point do you begin to feel nervous or even fear? Holding another person's eye contact can also appear aggressive except of course in intimate situations. Remember to handle this exercise sensitively.

If you are a woman you have an added hazard. Whether you like it or not if you catch a strange man's eye and hold it, it may be seen either as a 'come on', or truly aggressive. The problem arises if, even for an instant, you fancy them. Instinctively your pupil will grow larger and he will unconsciously respond to that signal. I always say to the groups to whom I am talking that it pays to lower your eyes or only look at him briefly until you have made your mind up! Otherwise you may have given a message you might regret later.

Body movements

When we communicate, body movements play an important part in giving messages. As you pick up messages about other people, so they understand things about you. If, for instance, you strongly disapprove of something said to you, you will draw back or fold your arms and if you do not wish to look aggressive, you may find an excuse to get up and move away.

It pays you to look carefully at your own body movements and become aware of them. They may have just become habits. You might want to change behaviour patterns which are distracting or revealing. We can all probably recall someone who annoys us by their habits or movements. Sometimes these movements seem to be catching and you even find yourself compulsively imitating them.

It can be useful to see yourself on video. Although you might find it embarrassing, at least it makes it possible to be honest with yourself about your habits. Alternatively you could ask a good friend to tell you about your faults (as well as your strengths). How do you hold yourself? Take a good look at yourself in front of a full-length mirror. How do you stand? Try the normal body stances you adopt. When trying to get on the same level as everyone else, tall people often stoop, while small people puff themselves up – both of which can give the wrong impression.

If you looked out once more at yourself through that mirror would you even think you looked aggressive? Practise a few non-threatening ways of standing. Keep a check on yourself as you go about your daily life. Watch out for yourself as you rap your knuckles, hammer a point home with a pointed finger, dismiss a person with the toss of your head or shrug of your shoulders. You may be surprised at how you can appear to others. Of course, once again it is a two-way affair. Watch other people as well.

There are complications here too. Different nationalities reflect their thoughts with body movements which can be quite distressful for others who are not on the same wavelength. We all know the obvious. The French appear to be very expressive with their shoulders and hands, the Turks can seem dismissive, the Chinese and Japanese can look as though they hardly react. However this is the picture which the English see, what view do other nationalities have of the English? In this multi-cultural society which is Britain today, we still do not seem to have tried to understand each other's non-verbal language and yet it is one of the ways by which we continue to make judgments of all those we meet. If we are not aware of this our responses can be quite inappropriate.

Body contact

It is through body contact that we express a large range of meaning, from the close proximity of lovers to the fleeting contact of shaking hands with a stranger. Once again there are unspoken unwritten rules about body contact which vary between cultures. For example, the French often kiss each other. Turkish men not only kiss each other but walk with their arms around each other, which in Britain would not be thought appropriate behaviour.

Touch has an important communicating role, showing encouragement, concern and emotional support. It can be used to help people who are in distress, anxious or are having difficulty articulating their feelings.

However, you always need to be aware that some people may be distressed by touch. They may feel sexually threatened or they may have unpleasant memories of being touched. A woman who has been sexually assaulted or harassed may be distressed by body contact, especially if it comes from a man. You need to take your cue from the non-verbal language you will be receiving.

Orientation

The distance between you and another person is very important and the position you adopt will affect the relationship between you.

Sitting side by side is seen as co-operative, whereas sitting opposite implies competitiveness and can be seen as authoritarian (eyeball-to-eyeball confrontation). For conversation or consultation it is best to sit at a ninety-degree angle, preferably with no desks or barriers in between. In the workplace many offices are almost set out with in-built aggression in that desks can only be fitted so that people sit opposite each other. This needs to be considered at the design stage.

It helps to keep down the likelihood of aggression if you sit at the same level or even a little lower than the other person so they can feel superior or at least equal. To be on a higher level is seen as 'superior' and does not set the scene for good communication. Of course many managers use this ploy deliberately, especially if they are not confident in their own role.

Personal space

It can feel aggressive, even offensive, if someone comes too close to you (this of course does not apply to your loved ones or those you know very well). If people get too close you will start to lean backwards or move away. If you are followed until you are backed up against the wall, you feel really threatened.

Why do you feel like this? Around you, you have an area shaped like an egg with the pointed end in front. This is your body buffer zone. People have different sizes of body buffer zones and the angrier they are the bigger it becomes. When someone gets too close to you they are entering this private space. Anyone invading this mobile personal territory is threatening its occupier and will create immediate tension. Angry people, especially angry men, have larger body buffer zones than others and we need to be wary of this.

Proximity means how close people are to each other. You respond to an invisible line between yourself and others. If you are too far back the other person can feel inaccessible. Too close and the other person may become uncomfortable and try to move away. People can have differing optimum distances and what feels too close for one person may be fine for someone else.

When standing you can interact at a closer distance than when you are sitting for you move away easily if the situation becomes uncomfortable. A sitting distance of five to six feet is usual for work situations. When standing the distance can be as short as three to four feet.

Proximity also relates to status; often a person of higher status feels free to approach a lower-status person, but not vice versa. At work your boss may feel free to stand closer to you, as a worker, than you feel able to stand to your boss.

If you have to get too close to others as say on the tube, you tend not to face other people, turning sideways and avoiding eye contact. If accidental eye contact occurs, you probably quickly turn away. If someone stares, you begin to feel threatened.

If you were on an empty train or bus, it would feel very odd if someone were to sit beside you when plenty of other seats were available. In that sort of situation you often extend your private space, using something like a bag or a briefcase as a barrier between yourself and the other person. You see some men leaning back and stretching their legs out wide in front of them. This can force a person trying to make their way down the carriage to have to step over the barriers in their way. This is annoying to a man but can feel even more distressing to a woman.

Incidentally you use this kind of tactic in your private life too. When you are in a pub, for instance, you hold your glass in front of you at the distance to which you wish to keep the person to whom you are talking. If you look down and your glass is quite close you may well like that person more than you admit to yourself.

On the other hand you may be using that glass as a barrier between yourself and others you feel are crowding you. In defending your personal space, barriers can be set up which can hinder effective communication and interaction, you can then find yourself once more unwittingly in an aggressive situation.

Discover your own body 'buffer zone'. There are many conversations where you may have felt uncomfortable because a person is too close. This is often a particular problem for women who are not very good at protecting the space where they feel at ease. When you are talking to someone, move very slightly backwards and forwards until you establish your own 'right' place and can talk to the person in a relaxed way. Usually a tall person will want to stand nearer to someone than a small person who really identifies with the problem of having their space frequently encroached. It is physically uncomfortable to stop and assess nasty situations and this can stop you fully realizing how others are feeling.

Listening well

It is also very difficult to listen to someone when you feel crowded. Good listening is crucial in order to pick up clues about someone's intentions.

Personal territory

Personal territory refers to the wider areas in which you seek to establish a sense of security and belonging. All of us establish personal territory. It might be at home, where you may have a certain area which is seen as yours, or at work where you arrange your office in a way which makes you feel secure.

We all know what it feels like when our own personal space is invaded. Wherever it is, your desk, your table where you write letters, even the garden shed, if you find someone else there using your pen or your telephone, muddling around on your potting table, up go your hackles and you can almost feel your claws come out. That place is yours, yours alone and you certainly feel like protecting every centimeter.

Imagine how much worse this must be when the rent collector calls and you have no money to pay; the health visitor comes and you are worried about the mess the baby is in; when the garrulous office gossip comes in to sit on your desk. Even as the knock is heard on the door your muscles tighten and the territory invader puts you on the defensive. Everyone needs to be aware of this effect we can have on others but it is particularly important if your very job is in itself a potential threat.

Emotional Communication

Mood

We can indicate our feelings and receive an impression of another person's mood just from the way we hold our body. The way we sit or stand tells a great deal about our mood and confidence, as well as our perceived position in the pecking order of those around us.

People who are anxious may clench their hands, pull at their clothing, adjust their hair; may have difficulty sitting still, may frown and bite their lips or perform other nervous movements such as fiddling with a pen or watch. Someone who is depressed may sit slumped in a chair, looking downcast and refusing to respond to conversation, or they may appear over-bright and breezy, exhausting to be with. You receive a wide range of non-verbal information, probably more than you realize.

You also tell others about yourself, probably more than you wish to admit. You need to be sensitive to these aspects of communication and recognize that even before you speak you have probably conveyed messages that will have a fundamental impact on the other person.

You can contradict your spoken word. You may be saying 'No' and nodding your head to indicate, 'Yes', or saying, 'I want to do this' but shaking your head to say, 'No'.

You might also be saying 'I feel fine' when your whole body shows that you are tense and anxious. You can show discrepancies between your eyes and mouth, so that when you smile your eyes stay dull. When these contradictory messages appear it is said to be the non-verbal message which is telling the truth. However we have to be aware of different cultural codes. It took me some time to realize that this was sometimes a cultural 'norm'. The Japanese people I was teaching to swim who were vigorously nodding their heads were responding firmly in the negative. I was getting a completely different message.

Try this exercise for yourself. For a couple of days keep taking a look at yourself. Every now and again have a look in a mirror, shop window or glass partition. Do you look as you feel? How do you feel? Do you spread gloom and doom or leave people all nervous and twitchy simply by reflecting your moods?

Why not experiment? Whatever you feel like, make an effort to appear confident and pleasant, open but not over-friendly; concentrate on how the other person is feeling. You may well find that the interesting reactions you receive will make you feel actively better. I remember someone telling me he had tried this once on someone who he always regarded as grumpy and hard to get on with. Before long he began to be impressed at how much this difficult person had changed. It took him some time to realize that the true picture was the reflexion of his own efforts!

Role play

We all take on many different 'roles' during our lives. Some of the roles we are expected to play are thrust upon us or we find ourselves undertaking them quite unexpectedly. Filled with nervous inexperience we can bluff our way through, pretending even to ourselves that we can cope. However occasionally this can lead us into problems and unaware of our blunders we can wonder what on earth went wrong.

I wish I had known for instance that a mother laying down the law with a 'do as I say!' demand will never calm down a tantrum throwing toddler. Instead the situation will be much more likely to escalate. When I had three children under three my exhaustion and dismay often found me in such a situation. Of course eventually commonsense helped me to learn but as I have said before my experience has also taught me that commonsense is so very rarely common practice.

Here I am reminded of the 'flying sink'. I learnt this story while I was speaking to a conference of housing officers. One of the occupants of a block of flats continually made complaints, the latest of which was the overflow of his sink. He rang up repeatedly and was always told that the telephonist would 'pass the message on'. Being a man of brute strength but few words, the man one day reached the end of his tether. He ripped the sink from the wall and carried its bulk down to the Housing Department. 'What', he shouted to the young temporary receptionist, 'are you going to do about this?' he bellowed, plonking the sink on her desk. 'It says here', the girl replied, falling behind jargon, 'that you cannot come without an appointment. There's no one who can see you at this moment,' and pointing to the offending sink she declared, 'Please remove this object and bring it back on Monday.' 'I bloody won't,' he yelled and picking it up he threw it full blast at the wall with such force that bits of it ricocheted around the open plan office hurting several people and causing much destruction on its way.

If she too had been aware that a pointing finger and, 'do as I tell you' attitude (like a dictatorial parent) will never be on the same wavelength as a tantrum throwing childlike person, the receptionist could have changed the situation completely.

Had she said, 'Oh dear, I can see you really do have a problem,' she would have represented (in TA – Transactional Analysis language) a 'caring parent'. If she had then said, 'Do put your burden down, sit with me, we will see what we can do,' the receptionist would then have moved the behaviour of both of them into the adult mode. When people discuss a subject in a logical rational way it is almost impossible for either side to become aggressive.

Everyone, whatever their IQ, can behave in the adult mode, unless they are psychotic, alcoholic or on drugs. If we always acted as adults we would be very boring; we need to have 'directional parents' in us so we can make up our minds; 'caring parents' in us so we can care for ourselves (unless we do, we cannot care for others); tantrums are sometimes a good idea, and the child in us contributes our sense of humour, wonder and flashes of brilliance. We need all parts to be a whole.

However when we take on a role: executive, carer, director or part of a team we need to ensure that we can vary the parts we play to suit the situation or we can once again allow unnecessary problems to arise.

In the case of the 'flying sink' the offender just wanted to communicate his frustration and his need. No one was listening to him. Unfortunately his demonstration almost led to demolition.

Social behaviour
From a very early age, perhaps from the moment we are born, we are socialized – that is, we learn behaviour which adapts us to life in the world around us including roles which label us 'female' or 'male'.

Girls have dolls, boys have cars. Girls unlike boys are not discouraged from crying but also, are expected to learn the role of 'carer': fetching the plaster and cleaning up a wound, cooking the meal, mending the sock, doing the shopping. Many women also learn that they have the privilege of having a door opened for them, of going first into a room, of being helped into a car and many other small politenesses. In the workplace however such actions can now become very dangerous. Our social behaviour may no longer have a place in our working lives.

As far as can be understood, Suzy's social behaviour let her down. Suzy followed her normal pattern that working day. She showed that man into a house which was empty. She unlocked the door and automatically preceded her client. With the door shut behind them she would have been trapped. It may well be that you should rethink your behaviour patterns and be aware of those which could lead you into trouble.

Ask yourself a few questions:
* Can you identify certain people who make you feel hostile/ angry?
* What is it about them which upsets you?
* Do you make people angry sometimes? Why do you think that is?
* When you have done this discuss your answers with a friend and see what thoughts and feelings you have in common and where you differ and why.

Controlling your emotions

We need our emotions to deal with both our own feelings and those of other people. Many of us have somehow fallen into the trap of thinking that the emotionally stable person is the one who never shows any emotions. Of course the opposite is nearer the truth. Emotions are resources which we should use, allowing ourselves to show love, affection, concern, and sorrow. Indeed repressing such emotions can result in us 'blowing our top', impair harmony, our logic and decision-making skills.

Overwhelming or inappropriate emotional responses can be destructive in more ways than one. Stress, physical fatigue, illnesses and chemical abuse can all hinder our own self-control.

It is the appropriate use and control of emotions which is our vital aid in our communication with others. It is well worth practising. However, as was shown in the chapter on Anxiety, strong emotions build up chemicals in the body especially when they are repressed. Work these out with the help of exercise and other activities. This will help keep you fit as well as 'let off steam'.

Laugh and the world laughs with you!
This is not easy because we all know we look stupid at times and most of us hate making fools of ourselves involuntarily. However there is a world of difference in being laughed 'at' and laughing 'with'. Once you have learned that you can laugh at yourself without losing face, the strength you will gain is enormous.

If we could not have laughed together at some of the pointless, wrong or even hideously cruel things people wrote and said in the media about us and those we loved, we would have gone mad. However, I think the key word here was 'us'. It does help to have others with whom you can talk, laugh and who understand. In that way you help each other's confidence and can grow in your ability to take chances. In fact most people admire those who do their best – and none of us can do better than that!

Self-worth is vital
Knowing that you really are as good as other people gives you the ability to stand up tall and face the world with clarity and without fear. We all have gifts and abilities which differ greatly but in our own way each one of us is intelligent, capable and equal to anyone else.

Comparing ourselves with others can be invidious and self-destructive. Take account of yourself, your talents, capabilities and situation and within these limitations give yourself the freedom to be and do what suits you best.

Value yourself for who you are and not what you might be. It was a great help to me when I learned that when someone 'accuses you of being or doing something' that it is usually the

accuser who is making a self-revelation about themselves. I
have tried this maxim out now on many occasions and found it
to be very true. Now I examine any accusation, look at it,
discuss with myself whether I need to 'take note'. If not I
metaphorically hand it back and think 'it's their problem – not
my problem' and refuse to take it on board.

If people laugh at you, criticize you, judge your behaviour,
stand to one side. Think of this as being someone else's
problem not your own. We can now get on with some positive
steps forward.

Distressing Communication

Harassment

Bullying and verbal abuse are very real forms of harassment
which can be debilitating to such an extreme as to physically
and emotionally destroy even the strongest spirit. Such
behaviour is rife and can be found in many workplaces –
banks, schools, hospitals, YTS schemes, offices, shops,
factories, prisons, the police – and in every walk of life. In
many cases people are so terrified into submission that the
problem remains largely concealed and no one recognizes that
it exists. Unfortunately in some environments it even seems to
be part of the ethos.

These forms of harassment are not confined to men but can
be equally perpetrated by women. Harassment may be the
result of various personal problems on the part of the
perpetrator. Many of these go back to some aspect of parent-
ing; someone who as a child was over-criticized or belittled
and given no encouragement, could resort to other ways to
gain power and exercise control over others using familiar role
models and expectations demanded of them. Alternatively the
victim could be more popular, better qualified, good at the
same job, a more socially well-equipped person than the
harasser.

Sometimes this behaviour is very subtle and the perpetrator never even realizes they are doing it. They believe it is accepted as 'humour', 'cleverness' or their right as a person in a higher position. Many even accept it as a male 'norm' and do not realize how insulting or dominating they are being.

However once the conscious harasser has found the 'chink in the victim's armour' whether it be reactions to aggressive tactics, lack of self-esteem, shyness about sex, defensiveness about being female/male or any particular race, the harasser will use every way to constantly wear the victim down. Some harassers do this to selected groups such as nurses, police, railway staff or a particular nationality. Harassers pick on the weaknesses of others. All harassers rely on a response from their victim to achieve success and encourage continuation of their bullying behaviour.

If a person does not know they are being harassed they are unaffected. Verbal, sexual or racial abuse can also fall unnoticed like water off a duck's back. But even if normally you do not react there is always the time when you are 'below par' and suddenly a shaft hits home. If you remember your own value and that their behaviour is their own problem not yours you will rise above the harassment and be able to cope with confidence.

However such harassment should never be allowed to continue for too long as it will gradually pollute the whole atmosphere. So what can you do?

If you are being bullied at work, the TUC advises members to contact their union representative. YTS advice is to report the facts to your local organizing office. Personnel staff are trained to deal with welfare problems in the workplace. One woman who was repeatedly bullied by her male boss advises: 'It is vital to watch out for others around you and to support them. Bullying is so insidious, before you realize it you're in it up to your neck.'

* Contact your union official, personnel officer, or, if you do not get their co-operation, someone higher in personnel or your union. You have the right to discuss the problem, in

confidence, with someone in authority, and you can ask for that person to be of the same sex as you.
* Talk to someone about the problem: friends, family, your immediate superior or your colleagues. You will no longer feel isolated and you may receive corroborative evidence.
* Ask the harasser to stop, either verbally or in writing; explain how their behaviour is causing you distress.
* Keep a diary of events (dates, times, locations, details of events, what was said, and so on). Collect evidence and keep a note of witnesses.

If your problem is at school go to the school nurse or counsellor. If you are at home or it's a neighbour (which is quite common) ask your local social worker if you can have a word with them as they may be able to refer you to someone who can help such as a tenancy relations officer or harassment unit. The most important thing is not to just sit there until you feel reduced to jelly. You will find that many people have endured such humiliation and will be very sympathetic. Join an assertiveness training course and you will meet many kindred spirits.

Sexual harassment

It will be no news to anyone that women have been subjected to sexual harassment at work for years – for far too long! Much of that harassment was, in my view, not so much for sexual purposes as for power used by men to try to maintain the male domination of their own perceived territory, or women to maintain control.

Sex discrimination is still a worrying and negative aspect of many occupations and it is much to the credit of women's organizations and the Equal Opportunities Commission that headway is beginning to be made. Much work has also been done by the TUC but I still wonder if they listen to their own rhetoric. When I address Trades Union Meetings there is hardly a female face to be seen let alone a single black or coloured one.

Sexual harassment does need to be taken seriously for a number of reasons:-

* Because it damages an employee's confidence and performance
* it creates an uncomfortable and intimidating working
  environment
* it seriously affects productivity, forcing women workers to
  take days off sick, seek transfers or even leave their job.

Although this is mainly a female problem, men can also have
considerable problems. When I first started to address groups
the ones I attended most were, of course, mainly from the
estate agency world. On one occasion a red-faced young man
asked the question, 'Tell me Mrs Lamplugh, what do I do
when I go to a house to measure up and give an estimation on
the market price and I am met by a woman in bra and pants
saying, "I am willing, waiting and wanting?" What do I do
then?' And it is true, how can he tell his peers, his boss, that he
has walked out, does not want to go back on his own again or
has perhaps even lost the sale? A woman would have no
problem in telling others.

Since those days I have heard similar stories from many
male 'out-workers', social workers, housing officers, surveyors, insurance salesmen. Such harassment takes place within
the workplace too. One of the reasons that women have been
able to be so bluntly active in this area is that they 'risk no loss
of face' by owning up to its existence. Men on the other hand
might well be seen as a wimp by both male and female
colleagues alike by not responding in the expected way. The
latest research by the LSE/Local Government Training Board
which The Suzy Lamplugh Trust instigated showed a high
incidence of under-reporting. However, it is vital that a man
should report such an incident. A rejected woman can be very
spiteful and make all sorts of allegations. It needs to be made
easier for men to talk without stigma about these experiences.

Sexual harassment is a problem that can be overcome. It is
an issue for all trade unionists – women and men.

The TUC defines sexual harassment as:

'Repeated and unwanted verbal or sexual advances, sexually explicit derogatory statements or sexually discriminat-

ing remarks made by someone in the workforce which are offensive to the worker involved, which cause the worker to feel threatened, humiliated, patronized or harassed, or which interfere with the worker's job performance, undermine job security or create a threatening or intimidating work environment.'

Sexual harassment can take many forms which include:-

* repeated and unwanted verbal or physical advances
* sexually explicit or discriminatory remarks
* unwelcome comments about person or dress
* requests for sexual favours
* offensive use of pin-ups, pornographic pictures etc.

It is important that we remember that sexual harassment is not the laughing matter it is so often portrayed to be by the media. Nor does working to eliminate sexual harassment mean an end to the fun and banter which should be part of every working environment and enjoyed by all.

Racial harassment

All the bullying, verbal abuse and sexual harassment sections apply here as well. Some racial harassment is due to jealousy, fear of the unknown and also the human instinct to 'pack up' on others to try and bolster their own collective fragile self-esteem.

However it is, as we all know much more than that, many of us simply do not understand each other. Our norms are not their norms, our priorities, ways of thinking can be quite at variance with those of other races and cultures. Nor is it simply confined to colour or parts of the world. We have great differences between regions in Great Britain too.

'Loss of face' in one country is so different for one race than another. I am very proud of my Welsh heritage. In our rural part of Wales there is no such thing as hierarchy, everyone is equal, anyone can be king for a day. This has in one way been an asset as I find no more problems in talking on a level with a Lord or Cabinet Minister than with a caretaker of a hostel for 'down-and-outs' in the Docklands. To me all are interesting, all are essential. However I realize now that in just charging on I have trodden on many sensibilities and stepped through many boundaries without a thought. This raises hackles, people become defensive of their perceived, acquired or required 'rights'.

I believe we all need to know more; we need to learn about each other's reasoning, cultures, gestures and unwritten rules. In the first place we should perhaps allow each other space without criticism. This might be a good start.

This is not to say that overt racial harassment and discrimination in the workplace should go unchecked. As with sexual harassment, the Equal Opportunities Commission and the TUC are doing very good work and the courts are now beginning to take it seriously. They deserve our support.

Communication Techniques

Getting your point across and allowing others to do the same is a fundamental part of communication. Much of the aggression we face in our daily lives is simply because of our failure to communicate with others on the same wavelength and without getting at cross purposes.

In the early part of 1985 in my role as Co-founder/Director of the British Slimnastics Association I attended a conference of the Sports Council. Writing in our in-house magazine in the Spring of 1986 I quoted from one of the speeches:-

'An adolescent needs to learn the essential difference between aggression which is to demolish and destroy, and assertion which is to overcome or triumph over opposition including oneself. Aggression can lead to personal demolition.'

This statement, made by a sports journalist, referred to football. At the time I applied it to exercise and relaxation. It is only since writing my book on *Beating Aggression* and then teaching our course on 'Coping with Aggression' to so many people working in vastly different workplaces and conditions, that I have come to fully realize the depth of understanding that this quotation reveals.

This statement does not only refer to youngsters, it applies to all of us. Aggressive people think only of themselves, whereas assertive people, knowing their own 'rights', can consider the views of others and make their own decisions without aggression and confrontation.

'Assertiveness training' is only one of a group of procedures used by behavioural and social therapists (psychologists, residential social workers, psychiatric nurses). It is particularly relevant and helpful for those who have difficulty standing up for themselves, making their feelings known and responding to other people's points of view. There are other procedures amongst this group of 'behavioural therapies' which may be more appropriate for other problems such as being too domineering, over-critical and hostile. These go by names such as 'Anger or impulse control' and are usually combined with 'Relaxation Training', to help people cope with the tension which arises from either anxiety or anger.

Assertiveness is useful because of its key importance in enabling people to make clear to others what they mean and what they want, and in considering what others mean and want. In the self-protection business it can be particularly effective in avoiding misunderstandings, being taken advantage of and possibly, in an unchecked extreme, becoming a victim of violence. However, we need to be careful not to imply that assertiveness is the solution to all personal effectiveness problems. In fact behavioural therapists would need to be sure they understood a person's whole background and needs and would then tailor the treatment to these, drawing upon probably several social skills or behavioural approaches.

I find that many men misunderstand the meaning of assertiveness. It is often seen as a purely female subject. This is quite untrue. Learning and practising assertive techniques can give great freedom and strength. Although it is not a panacea it is to be recommended for everyone, men and women alike.

Of course assertiveness techniques can also be an invaluable asset in other aspects of your life. Everyone's judgment, actions and reactions can be so complicated by emotional feelings that to truly help yourself improve your communication links in personal relationships, it is worth considering signing on to take part in a full assertiveness training course. The whole course does in any event cover a much wider vision than we can touch on here.

What is assertion?
When I ask this question of delegates on a training course they invariably describe someone who is being aggressive rather than assertive.

Aggression, since it means doing harm to others, can be seen as allowing yourself rights but denying any to the other person. Aggressive people think mainly of themselves and not of other people. The assertiveness approach involves respecting your own rights and those of others, and taking responsibility for yourself and allowing others to take responsibility for themselves. Getting your point across and allowing others to do so is a fundamental part of assertiveness.

Assertiveness does not guarantee that you will get what you want, but it is a 'Win-Win' situation in that both people are treated as equals and both are taken into consideration. I do not guarantee that the other person will always like you or be happy with your approach, but it does give them the opportunity to be taken seriously and to know where they stand with you.

Why be assertive?
The assertiveness approach is a positive approach both for you and for the people with whom you come into contact. Being assertive can help you, both at work and personally, in the following ways:

* You gain in confidence: Everyone gets stressed and has times when self-confidence goes. By deliberately using assertive methods you can help yourself deal with stress, keep your self-esteem from sinking and bolster your confidence when faced with a stressful situation. This does not mean that you become over-confident, but rather that you retain a balanced view of yourself. You can keep a realistic belief in yourself, your abilities, your value as a person and your rights, while acknowledging and accepting your faults and mistakes and trying to do something about them without punishing yourself.

* Controlling your anxiety: Assertive methods can help you to accept that it is all right to be human and have emotions such as anxiety, whilst also ensuring that anxiety does not take over.

* Becoming an assertive role model: By being assertive you can demonstrate to other people that there is an alternative to aggression, submission and being manipulative. In this way you make it easier for others to be assertive as well. This is important if your colleagues and friends are to develop their own assertiveness.

* Using anger constructively: Assertive methods will help you to express anger appropriately and to use the energy of anger to get things done, rather than suppressing it or dumping it on people who do not deserve it. It helps you keep your voice steady and your body language unthreatening so in lowering the tenor of the communication it can allow both sides to hear and understand each other.

* Long-term gains: Although plucking up the energy and courage to be assertive in difficult situations can at first cause increased short-term stress, in the long term you will have less stress and better working relationships (and personal ones too). You will be more effective in your work, whatever it is.

What are your rights?

Although I have the obligation to respect the rights of

others, I also have the right to receive similar respect from them – for instance:

I have the right to be treated with respect as an intelligent, capable and equal person.

I have the right to be listened to and taken seriously.

I have the right to ask for what I want.

I have the right to state my own needs and set my own priorities as a person, whatever other people expect of me.

I have the right to say 'No' without feeling guilty.

Now consider this one:

'I have the right to judge my own behaviour, thoughts and emotions and *take responsibility for their initiation and consequences.*'

The second half of the sentence is the balance. For instance if you have accepted a job, signed a contract and taken on the ethos and rules of that job, and if you then overtly exercise some of your rights you may put your job on the line. You may however decide that you wish to take on that responsibility or that it is important to do so because the principles on which you took on the job have been changed.

You always need to weigh up your decision to exercise your rights against any important possible consequence.

Reactions to assertiveness

Most of the time being an assertive person is quite straightforward, and so acceptance and easy communication are common reactions. You may be surprised at how often things go well. People know where they stand with you, they are less likely to misunderstand you, so they can feel secure with you. This means there is less overall anxiety and less chance of non-assertive reactions.

On the other hand, you will probably also encounter some non-assertive responses; some people find it hard to cope with an assertive approach at first and may persist in responding aggressively, submissively or in a manipulative way. However, if you have given them ample opportunity to respond assertively, their lack of assertiveness is not your responsibility. It may cause you problems, but then you would have had more problems with those people had you not been assertive.

Assertive body language

An assertive approach is reflected by more than the words that are spoken. Non-verbal communication is an important part of assertiveness. For example:

Posture: usually relaxed, relatively calm, well-balanced and upright, facing the other person at the same level and not moving unnecessarily.

Gestures: generally relaxed but, if indicating the strength of feeling behind what is being said, with open hands and not invading the other person's space.

Eye contact: direct but relaxed and at the same eye level as the other person, indicating a willingness to listen.

Facial expression: generally relaxed, firm, open and pleasant, without inappropriate smiles, displaying suitable strength of feeling. Indicates a willingness to listen on equal terms.

Voice: generally relaxed and low-pitched, with a firm gentle tone and enough volume to be heard clearly, though it may show an appropriate amount of emotion to indicate the strength of feeling behind what is being said.

Distance: a comfortable proximity, making it easy for the other person to respond.

Communicating with other people

As you will have realized by now we often muddle up our lines of communication to such an extent that it is easy to misinterpret and react inappropriately to each other. This gets even more complicated as we cross cultural barriers. We only have to look across the Channel and watch the different negotiating techniques to realize each and every one of us still has a great deal to learn. Nearer to home, management and trades unions also have their own techniques and these need to be understood to achieve any progress.

This is perhaps what makes it all so interesting. I hope you enjoy practising these communication techniques and exercises. You will not just learn them overnight; many of our fundamental rights have been battered out of us since birth. Please do plough on – it is more than worth it.

Gradually I hope you have been building up confidence in your own ability to manage aggression. In the next chapter we will take the final steps to dealing with real violence and creating our own action plan.

Confidence

Confidence comes from being aware of the actuality of the risks you may have to face; recognizing and responding to potential aggression or a real threat without debilitating fear; knowing when and how to mediate and protect yourself from attack; how and when to use physical restraint as a last resort when in real danger.

This chapter will:
- put your fear into perspective
- ensure you can be aware of the most useful responses to defuse aggression which may escalate to violence
- show you the 'First Aid' and 'Essential Aid' responses which are most likely to protect you from attack.

This chapter will cover:
- signs of potential violence
- responding to a threat
- mediating
- using physical control
- personal response to physical attack
- use of physical force and offensive weapons
- protecting yourself from attack
- attack responses
- sexual offences.

By the end of this chapter you should be able to:
- recognize a potential aggressor
- know how to react positively to an aggressor
- recognize unhelpful reactions you may be pre-programmed to respond with to defend yourself

- understand how you can 'walk straight into trouble' if you do not programme yourself to respond automatically with the action which will enable you to 'Get Away'
- realize that prevention is preferable to defence.

Confidence in yourself and your own ability to manage aggression comes from being aware of the real problems and knowing that you can draw on and put into practice self-protection techniques, strategies and skills. This book is not intended to be a 'Do as I say – or else' statement. The whole objective has been to present you with the facts and information to make 'Informed Choices' and the awareness of possible consequences of your decisions.

Throughout this book we have been gradually assessing your own personal risks and finding ways to further reduce any potential problems which you might encounter. All the time this book has emphasized that the risk you run of becoming a victim of true aggression or violence is very small.

To once more put the facts into perspective let's look at the *Which Report* on street crime published in November 1990. They used the British Crime Survey (bcs) facts as they felt it was a better indicator of published crime rates than police statistics because not all crimes are reported to, or recorded by, the police. Sexual offences are still particularly poorly reported – no reliable estimates exist. The bcs figures show:

* The likelihood of being mugged is considerably less, even in a 'high-risk' area than the one in five chance of your car, or something from it, being damaged or stolen in a year.
* Muggings are more common in inter-city, multi-racial areas, council estates with low-income tenants, and areas with 'non-family' housing – from bed-sits to large, expensive houses. These are classed as high-risk areas.
* Men are more at risk than women from crime overall and particularly of violent crime in the streets.

* Elderly people are less at risk of crime than young people, and not just because they go out less. It is young men who are most at risk from assault and robbery.
* Afro-Caribbean and Asian people are more likely to be victims of crime than whites.
* Asians are more likely to suffer vandalism, personal theft and victimization by groups of strangers.

So, statistically I am afraid, if you are Afro-Caribbean or Asian and a young man you are most at risk. However, none of us can in my view be complacent nor can we run away from the fact that this certainly seems to be becoming a more and more violent society.

A friend visiting her father in hospital the other day reported to me that several of his fellow patients were victims of violence.

* One was returning to his new house where he was busy painting a ceiling, having just seen his wife off in their car to go shopping, he was attacked by a strange man who was standing in his hall. Although frozen to the spot he did manage to lift his arm to shield his face but was left with twenty-six stab wounds down his body.
* Another man, returning home slightly merry from a golf club party swung his raffle prize of a bottle of port backwards and forwards with pleasure, when he was attacked by four youths as he walked down a dark alley to his house.
* One more was a security man who jumped in front of a robber's get-away car and was literally run over for his trouble.

I hope by now that you could:

* look at these cases and assess the risks these men ran
* analyse the strengths they could have put into action
* realize what you might have done in similar circumstances.

It seems sensible to me that we could do even more to increase our personal safety; we can take some positive steps to help ourselves. However low the apparent risk it would be folly for us to believe that we are invincible, to kid ourselves that, 'it will never happen to us'. We need to look at how to recognize, respond to and deal with real violence. Realizing our strengths and limitations will bolster our confidence even more and that in turn helps us to appear and therefore be less vulnerable.

Recognizing a Threat

If you are scared or even uneasy – do not ignore it, act on it straightaway.

Your anxiety is a better indicator of something threatening than looking for signs of anxiety in others.

Fear is information for you to use, therefore if the hair stands on end up the back of your neck, your heart misses a beat or your guts twist up, stop and assess. It may be only a natural reaction to change or the unknown, or it may be a real danger.

Signs of Potential Violence

The following symptoms in another person *may* indicate the onset of violence:

* agitation and threatening statements or gestures
* clenched fists
* gritted teeth
* pounding of fists on the table or other objects
* loud, harsh speech
* obvious muscle tension in face, hands and limbs

* high level of activity such as rapid walking, wringing of hands or frequent shifting of position
* inability to cope with stress
* impulsiveness
* paranoid statements
* headaches
* dizziness

It is helpful to note the colour of the potential aggressor's face. If someone is pale, he is more dangerous than if he has reddened. Pallor is part of the 'action system' and means that the body is prepared either to fight or to flee. A pale person approaching menacingly really is likely to attack.

If however he has turned bright red, he is no longer in the initial state of readiness. This sort of person, who will probably explode with roars and curses, may seem alarming but he is in fact demonstrating that 'his bark is worse than his bite'. But beware of being too complacent! He may revert to pallor and attack.

Never Minimize a Threat

When you are frightened ask yourself:

- Is this person's anger/hostility directed at me, the organization or themselves? Is it a form of distress?
- Are you in danger? If you think you are, leave and get help immediately.
- Are you the best person to deal with this? If you find particular situations difficult, perhaps someone else could handle it more effectively. This is a positive step *not* a cop-out!

Responding to a Real Threat in a Trapped Situation

If the threat of violence is imminent, avoid potentially dangerous locations such as tops of stairs, restricted spaces or where there is equipment which could be used as a weapon.

Keep looking for potential escape routes; for instance try to make sure you are between the aggressor and the door, if possible behind a barrier such as a desk.

Never turn your back. If you are leaving move gradually backwards.

Never remain alone with an actively violent person. Be prepared to move very quickly if necessary.

If you manage to calm the situation down, very slowly re-establish contact. Take care with your words and actions, making a gradual approach.

Never forget that your aim in an increasingly aggressive situation is to leave the scene if at all possible.

Walk away from real danger.

Remember that aggression meeting aggression adds up to confrontation.

Your primary aim should always be to get away.

Carry a *Suzy Lamplugh Alarm*, swung up by an aggressor's ear it can be used as a deterrent and if you press it down firmly and throw it to one side, the continuing horrendous scream will divert most attackers and attract help.

It helps to know your environment, to be AWARE, ALERT and AVOID trouble, defending yourself only if really necessary.

Mediating

We also need to develop skills in handling different situations because you may decide that mediation is the right option to deal with a problem or to prevent it from becoming more explosive, or because you have no option, such as when locked in, prevented from leaving or even held hostage. These skills can be of use too with those persons who already are or will be actually violent or are known to have been so in the past.

Before you choose this option ask yourself:

Is your breathing rapid or shallow?
Is your voice too loud, croaking or high-pitched?
Is your heart rate fast, are your palms beginning to sweat?

Do the *Quick Action Response Tension Release* exercises and breathe out slowly. This will calm you down, enable you to think and be ready for action.

Do not respond aggressively. This will increase the chance of confrontation.

Stay calm, speak gently, slowly and clearly. Do not argue or be enticed into further argument (this will not be easy as aggression does tend to lead to anger in others).

Do not hide behind your authority, status or jargon. Tell them who you are, ask the person's name, and discuss what you want him or her to do.

Try to talk things through as reasonable adults, in order to defuse the situation but remember your first duty is to yourself.

Avoid an aggressive stance – crossed arms, hands on hips, a wagging finger or a raised arm – these will only challenge and confront. Keep your distance and try to avoid looking down on your aggressor.

Never put a hand on someone who is angry, wait until they are completely calm.

A person on the brink of physical aggression has three possible choices: to attack, retreat or compromise. You need to guide them towards the second or third. Encourage the person to move, to the toilet, for a walk, to see a colleague. Offer a compromise such as talking through the problem or divert the aggression into such actions as allowing/encouraging banging on a table or tearing up paper.

DO:-	DO NOT:-
– the Quick Action Response Tension Release	– be too nervous
– be in control of yourself	– appear to expect attack
– project a calm, assured feeling	– be bossy
– pitch voice low/normal	– let voice be high pitched
– look at chest . . . eyes	– stare
– talk with the aggressor	– threaten
– listen	– argue
– be polite	– show emotion
– ensure others know where you are	– tense up
– seat subject	– corner
– sit yourself at right angles at the same level or slightly lower	– give up
– keep hands free	– Put hands in pocket

Always control yourself before controlling others. Talk yourself down mentally, breathe properly.

Using Physical Control

The use of physical restraint by one member of the public on another should be avoided unless there is a real danger and absolutely no other alternative. Certain professionals such as the police and security employees are highly trained and fit enough to deal with such tricky situations. But for most of us the best move is to run away to make a phone call to get aid rather than weigh-in, full of good intention but most likely out of your depth.

Prison officers, psychiatric nurses and others in similar professions may have to physically control people if they become disturbed to the extent that they are about to be a danger to staff and others. Effective action needs on-the-spot judgment born of considerable background knowledge in the particular area involved. As I have travelled around the country since the formation of The Suzy Lamplugh Trust giving talks to women's groups, unions, Rotary, youth clubs, schools, or training to police, prison officers, magistrates clerks, caretakers, hospital workers and so many more, it is obvious to me that each place has its own problems and solutions. Hotels are not the same as pubs; bingo halls are different from building societies; estate agents cannot learn much from retail or Council housing departments.

Risk situations should be prevented wherever possible. A great deal of work in this area has been done by the Health and Safety Executive Committee on Violence. One of the most valuable methods seems to be to have working video cameras which can monitor risk areas. These recordings can be used as workshop material for security managers, personnel officers and employees to work out the best ways to avoid such incidents occurring again. These methods then need to be assessed, reassessed, and continually monitored to ensure everyone involved is in agreement and kept up to date.

Personal Response to a Physical Attack

Self-defence is legally only allowed in certain circumstances. Remember aggression meeting aggression adds up to confrontation. In any violent physical contact, everyone will get hurt.

Remember if you are attacked you have three options:

Attack   Flight   Compromise

It is obviously safer for you to choose the last two!

Remember. Self-defence will not turn you into a person who does not have to avoid risks. The techniques are almost impossible to learn from books, they need 'hands on' training and to be regularly practised. However much training you have there are always times when you will not be on top form.

Even if you undertake a course at your Adult or Further Education classes, Leisure Centre or Recreation Club beware of being so confident that you forget to take care.

Use of Physical Force

It is good law and good sense that a person who is attacked may defend themselves, but you may only do what is reasonably necessary. Everything will depend upon the particular facts and circumstances.

In some cases it may be only sensible to take some simple avoiding action. You can never know how serious an attack will become.

If it were a relatively minor attack it would not be common sense to allow retaliation which was wholly out of proportion to that necessary in the situation.

If an attack was over and no sort of peril remained then the use of further force could be judged as revenge or punishment.

Whether the force used was judged to be reasonable, would be a matter for a jury if anyone brought a charge.

What is reasonable?
The judgment of 'reasonable' would result if the jury thought that in a moment of unexpected anguish a person attacked had only done what he honestly and instinctively thought necessary.

An assault is a crime; anyone going to the rescue of someone being assaulted, would be judged as using force to prevent crime, providing the force used was reasonable.

Defence of Property

Reasonable force to defend your property is lawful, the same principles apply as to self-defence.

Offensive weapons

Here is a quote from the Metropolitan Police:

> 'Under the Prevention of Crime Act 1953 it is an offence for any person to have with him in a public place an offensive weapon.
>
> An offensive weapon is any article which is made or adapted for use in causing injury or intended by the person having it with them for such use by him or some other person.
>
> It is not a "reasonable excuse" in law to claim you carried the weapon to use because you considered the streets were unsafe.'

Articles with blades or points

Under the 1953 Prevention of Crime Act a person having an ordinary knife in their possession was committing no offence. However, even though the possession of the knife was innocent they may well resort to using it as a weapon 'in the heat of the moment'.

Parliament therefore decided that it was desirable to deter people from carrying articles in public places, which are capable of being used for cutting or stabbing even though there was no intention or no evidence of intention at the time they were being carried for this purpose. Therefore Section 139 Criminal Justice Act 1988 states that any person who has any article which has a blade or is sharply pointed (except a folding pocket knife with a blade cutting edge of 3" or less) with him in a public place, shall be guilty of an offence.

If, however, the article with a blade or point was either

made, adapted or intended for use to cause injury it would be an 'offensive weapon' under the PCA 1953 (even the folding pocket knife with a blade less than 3").

These laws do not preclude the use of innocent items to defend yourself, providing that the force used is reasonable.

Keys, hairspray, comb or umbrella or a handbag etc. normally retained for innocent use and used in the heat of the moment could be alright providing their application was reasonable.

Protecting Yourself from Attack

Just pause for a moment and ask yourself:

'How could you protect yourself, now this minute – considering what you have with you, on you or within you – should you be about to be attacked?'

I pose this question when I speak to groups around the country. It never ceases to amaze me that no matter who makes up the group, whether they are young or old; male, female or mixed; managers or cogs in a wheel; white collar or no collar at all workers; or those groups of people who often have to work the hardest of all and yet refer to themselves as 'only' a housewife or househusband; all these people come up with a remarkably limited list of ideas. When we discuss these together many of these responses would in fact have probably led them into further trouble.

I do not lightly call this my 'debriefing' session (though I quickly realized my choice of words might have been slightly better chosen for a mainly male audience of Prison Officers at a Scottish gaol!) So much of our knowledge on this subject of self-defence seems to be gleaned from ill-considered sources and half-heard, vaguely-understood media presentations. Some of our responses can be pre-programmed by poor teaching based on Martial Arts Sports, Armed Force combat training or the police ability to fell a burglar. Many of these instructions lead people to be over-confident and yet quite unprepared when the real threat happens.

The majority of us, if we can operate at all and have not frozen with fear or lashed out without conscious thought, take the first action we have pre-thought ourselves to make.

Let's look at these in more detail:

Shoes I always know which people are going to suggest this. I can see, by their animated movements to each other, their intentions and perhaps even excitement at the very thought of being 'allowed' to have a go!

'What do you intend to do with your shoes?'
'Grind my heel into his instep'
'Kick him in the knees'
'Let him have it where it hurts'

they say with their eyes glinting!

'What is our aim?' I ask everyone and the replies are numerous – to hit him back, make it hurt, defend myself. I ask them again:
'What is our aim?'

Eventually we arrive at the answer. *Our aim is to get away.*

To do this we are going to need to be prepared to move, move quickly and without difficulty. This will mean wearing shoes which enable us to do this. The most important thing about our shoes is that they should fit. It is almost impossible to run well with one shoe on and one shoe off. Treading on a sharp object with bare feet might be disastrous.

Comfortable, well-fitting shoes with heels that are not too high are the ideal. For myself, I have decided to join the Americans. It delighted me when I realized, on a visit to Florence, that all the tourists from the USA were wearing their trainers along with their best clothes. To the uninitiated eye they did look slightly odd, especially accompanied by their bright socks. Nevertheless I joined them and at last had a sightseeing, gallery-walking holiday with feet which did not hurt and spoil the occasion. I now wear these shoes when out and about in what I perceive to be dodgy areas. Not only can I walk comfortably, but I have confidence in my ability to move quickly, if necessary. I make a quick change of shoes on arrival at any official function and so never feel out of place there either.

Nor would I suggest that you 'knee him in the groin'. Looking at the excited faces in front of me I often wonder if many people have a secret urge to be 'given leave' to inflict this kind of pain and injury! However, it will usually be ineffectual. Under tension men will unconsciously withdraw their private parts to protect them; they will be far too high up to reach!

There is an added risk too. Muggers – for those are the greatest number of attackers – go for easy game. If you lift one leg to strike upwards, kick out at a shin, lash back at a knee, you will be off balance and a literal 'push over' to someone who will already have the advantage of surprise and will usually be bigger and heavier.

Your first thought should be to get those legs moving. Walking fast is most appropriate as it does not escalate a situation. But, if necessary, run; getting and keeping fit is a very good aid to self-protection.

Fingers/pen/sharp object These ideas always come up. 'What do you intend to do with your fingers?' I ask. Answers come from all round the room. 'Poke them in his eyes'. I then ask, 'How many of you have ever thought of gouging out anyone's eyes lately?'

The faces reflect their feelings of disgust and revulsion except for one or two who gleefully say, 'I have'. 'And have you done it?' I counter.

These moves have often been taught in so-called 'self-defence' classes. They are even seen in videos, books and magazines. However, the fact is that psychologically we have an inbuilt inability to inflict such a wound. I met one person who tried to do this and she said, 'I suddenly thought, he's some mother's son'. That assailant caught hold of her arm and twisted her over on to her back.

If our first thought is go for the eyes, we may lift our hand, but immediately we look at the attacker's eyes we recognize them as a fellow human being. Unless we are trained like the SAS, police or the military, our normal reaction will be to hesitate and try to withdraw. We have then given our hand to the assailant to use as a useful lever against ourselves.

Nor would it be at all easy to put our fingers up his nostrils. They managed to get the chips in place in *A Fish Called Wanda*, but only because the victim's hands were tightly tied and I imagine even then it took a number of 'takes'.

The only place you could reasonably manage would be under the cheekbone, but this is a final resort and I will give you more thoughts about that at the end of this section. Basically it comes back to our aim. Do not stop, do not hesitate – get away as quickly as you can.

Bash him with my bag/briefcase is another thought. However, this is not as easy as it sounds. As we have discussed before, in an attack situation we are apt to tense up and that includes the hand gripping our bag or briefcase. Also, the chances are that this is the possession the mugger really wants; your clamped grasp can lead to a tug-of-war or even being dragged along so you become really injured.

It is easy to say you will give your bag up to the mugger but not so easy to actually do it. Make sure you do not carry your 'whole life' around with you, like your filofax. Keep some money on your person in an inaccessible place. Your bag is not worth being hurt for – be prepared to give it away.

I recently met a man who was attacked by four men who wanted his briefcase. It was in broad daylight and he was making his way to the studios where he was a producer. He said he should have realized that they were about to gang up on him but it was only in retrospect that he recognized the signs.

At the time he just hung on to his case for all he was worth. He said he remembered thinking, 'It's mine, how dare they!' but then he found himself knocked to the ground, and so shocked that even weeks later he was occasionally found sitting in his office with tears pouring down his face. Post-trauma reactions are very real and need long-term help and support. Taking evasive action should become a way of life.

'*My keys, my keys*' are another favourite option and I am shown a keen knuckleduster. 'What's the best use of your keys?' I ask infuriatingly, and a vicious punch forward is the demonstrative reply. We go back to the aim – if we genuinely want to get away the best use of our keys is to open the door behind which we will be more secure. So the key we will need to have ready is the first one we need, whether it is for our car, our office or our home. It is no good fumbling with our key ring under tension. Of course, if holding the bunch of keys in your hand also gives you the confidence of having added power available that is well and good. Confident behaviour is your best ally.

'*My shriek alarm*' is a good answer, but where is it? Often the person dives into their bag and scrabbles around among the paraphernalia of a lifetime. Any alarm is useless unless it is immediately available. You cannot hold up your hand and ask the mugger to hold on a minute while you look. It needs to be ready there and then! Remember, you should bring it up sharply by the attacker's ear (either front or back). Do not hesitate to see if he is alright – your instinct is to ask if he is OK! Immediately run away and ensure you report it to the police. Walking along, knowing where you are going, having pre-thought your route, in comfortable fitting shoes, carrying your keys in one hand and an alarm (if you feel the occasion warrants it), will enable you to walk with a sense of purpose and awareness that nine times out of ten helps keep you out of trouble.

Attack

If you are trapped and your instinct is that fighting back might work, then fight with as much anger as you can and without constraint. Remember this is your life and it is worth fighting for: claw at the face, go for the windpipe, go for wherever it may hurt. Do not worry about hurting your attacker; you must get free:

- The solar plexus (in the 'V' in the chest area between the ribs) is a vital striking area. It is the centre of a web of nerves and a forceful blow with an elbow, umbrella or walking stick has a paralyzing effect. The attacker will feel a deep sense of nausea so intense that even a drunkard or a person high on drugs can be stopped.
- The elbow joint is also very weak. A strike on the elbow joint with the palm of your hand when the attacker's arm is straight is very painful and disabling.
- Under the armpit, slightly to the front is a very vulnerable spot. It is an area rich in nerves and arteries and a walking stick, umbrella point, key or ballpoint pen jabbed here causes intense pain.
- The large area running down the side of the rib cage. Any blow here can be painful. A palm or side of the hand, a bunch of keys, a pencil or pen, stick or umbrella, even a hardback book, especially if the strike is hard, will cause great pain.
- Try twisting the ears off or shout down them; slap both sides of the head. A sharp quick strike *between* the eyes can knock your attacker unconscious. If your life is in danger, strike hard.
- The fingers. Bend any finger right back (not just a little way). Stamp on them, bite them, pull them apart. A broken finger is completely disabling.

Disable your attacker and then leave the scene. If you do manage to free yourself, run away immediately. Do not stop to have one more go at him or to see what you have done. The idea is to 'bash' and 'dash'.

Post-trauma Reactions

It is easy to toss off an attack, especially when we are not badly physically affected. However, the current statistics show that this can be much more long term and debilitating than had been previously thought. The organization, Victim Support, have been giving superb help in this field and their work is widening and increasing all the time. You can find them in your local phone book. Employers, too, have begun to recognize the need for post-trauma courses.

There are, however, the more insidious, but nonetheless most destructive forms of aggression such as verbal abuse, sexual and racial harassment as well as bullying. The trades unions have been working hard in these areas in the workplace to good effect. If your problem is at home consult your nearest Citizen's Advice Bureau.

Sexual Offences

As we have seen, the incidence of sexual offences are, comparatively speaking, very low. They can however be very serious and also affect many young boys and men as well as girls and women. If you are a victim the primary thing to remember is that it is *not* your fault. It is important to report it, otherwise others, including yourself, may suffer even more. Most rape cases are within the home. (Rape within marriage is an actionable offence.) The 'first date' rape is the next most common offence and I always warn people against going home with or inviting home anyone on first acquaintance however well they claim to be known or connected with friends or your family. The 'first date' rapist is often charming. It is impossible to believe they mean ill, to such an extent that you may be forced into believing you are responsible, or somehow 'asked' for what happened.

Make it a rule to never go home with or invite into your home a man you have just met. If they are alright there will always be another time.

Many of us have seen 'flashers' at some time or another. There is a natural tendency just to take fright and scurry on your way. The police, quite rightly, would like us to report such an incident so they can begin to build up a profile. There is a growing school of thought which ties in sexually abused children to juvenile offenders who may become flashers, who can go on to rape or even worse. It is very important to interrupt this vicious cycle.

The most difficult thing for you is that the details the police will want are of the man's face and quite honestly it is unlikely to be the part of the anatomy to which your eyes are drawn! However, if you can look up at the face and consequently give a good description you may be of invaluable help to others.

Conclusion

All through this book we have been discussing how you can take responsibility for your own safety. As you will have seen there is a great deal you can do. However, I am well aware that putting all the onus on you as an individual is not good enough. There are many others who should carry their responsiblities too.

Whose Responsibility?

In April 1988 the Trust ran a conference at London University entitled 'Aggression and Violence at Work'. It was opened by John Patten, the Minister of State at the Home Office concerned with crime prevention, and we invited everyone we felt would or should have an interest in this subject.

In my opening remarks to this conference I posed a question:

'Who should accept responsibility for aggression and violence in the workplace?' Who should, as the Trades Unions say, claim 'ownership' of this problem?

I told the delegates about my visit to the village where a young newspaper boy had just been murdered. I went up to Hagley to talk, not to the parents, but to all the friends and relations and all the community who were so shocked, disturbed and bereft that the little boy was killed. He was just doing his job.

Whose responsibility was that?

Was it the responsibility of the Employer who was employing a thirteen-year-old boy to go down a road which is very badly lit?

Or perhaps, the Local Authority's responsibility for allowing such a young boy to be employed in that area?

Was it the Environment Committee's responsibility in leaving this as a very dangerous road where anybody could have been picked up? And where there were a number of bushes everywhere?

Was it the Education Authority – was the boy educated properly to deal with that kind of problem?

Whose problem was it? Where should the responsibility lie?

Shouldn't we *all* be taking responsibility? Responsibilities, like explanations, seldom rest on only one person or factor, although media and public alike invariably think or make out they do.

It appeared, from the feedback from the group discussions which took place on that day in April 1988, that:

- the Environment Group felt that the Government should accept responsibility;
- the Local Authorities felt everyone should play a part, but they worried about the money;
- the Media were quite sure it was the responsibility of the Education Authorities;
- Education Authorities knew that the main responsibility should be more reporting of incidents;
- the Unions felt everyone should accept ownership of the problem, not only within the workplace but also travelling to and fro;
- the Employers, recognizing that care of employees was cost-effective, were prepared to accept their responsibility but were searching for ways and means . . .

One year later a great deal had been achieved. It was good to report that a number of major initiatives were clarifying the issues and providing increasing support and help. It was only in March, 1989, that the Trust published its research by the LSE (sponsored by Reed Employment) showing the hard statistics, but the subject was already considered to be very real indeed.

In February 1989, at the Health and Safety Executive's conference on 'Violence in the Workplace', run by the Executive's Committee on Violence (on which I represent the Trust), the HSE warned employers that if the recommendations in their new guidelines for employers are not implemented, the Government would not hesitate to enforce the measures by law.

We have come a long way since April 1988. Even so, the Conference report entitled 'A Living Agenda' makes fascinating reading. We still have much to do.

Since then I am glad to say there has been a great deal of progress. For instance, a number of major initiatives have been and continue to clarify the issues and provide increasing support and help. I can promise you that the Trust continues to prod and act as an irritant and catalyst as well as present some useful answers, guidelines, books, training courses and safety gadgets. Others too, such as Safer Cities Projects, the Health and Safety Executive, Crime Concern, the Community Action Trust and Victim Support, are doing some remarkable work and you will find a list of interesting projects, research, reading and useful addresses at the back of this book.

In the meantime let us look at the personal responsibility you can take if you wish to do so:

Accept reality
Put aside your preconceptions and take a clear look at the statistics. You may be more vulnerable than you thought. Be prepared to act accordingly. However, realize that confidence comes from being aware of the reality. This means:

- assessing the risks
- knowing your abilities
- realizing your strengths.

Be aware of potential problems
None of us is invincible – it is folly to kid yourself that 'it will never happen to you'!

Learn to trust your intuition: if you feel scared or even uneasy – do not ignore it, act on it *straightaway*.

Develop relaxation and tension control
If you are stressed or afraid, your feelings can escalate any aggressive situation. Regular practice is essential.

Be alert when out and about
Follow the plan when travelling on business or to and from the workplace.

Stand up tall, keep your feet slightly apart for good balance.

Keep your head up and your mind focused on your surroundings.

Know where you are going and how you are going to get there – look confident without appearing arrogant.

Go to exercise classes – good posture, stamina and strength are a positive aid to self-protection.

Avoid putting yourself at risk – follow sensible precautionary procedures
When you have to go out always leave behind you in writing details of where you are going and the time you expect to be back.

Assess potentially risky situations and avoid them if possible.

Be aware of problems at work
Your employer has a responsibility to provide directions and support for employees.

As an employee you have an individual responsibility never to put yourself, your colleagues, clients or members of the public at unnecessary risk.

The ideal is an atmosphere and procedures within the workplace where discussing fear and other problems is seen not as a mark of failure but as part of good practice.

Body language
Your 'body language' gives out signals which you may not intend but which are unconsciously sensed by others.

Personal space and territory
How to respect other people's personal territory; walking into

someone's territory can be an invasion of privacy and seem very threatening – even taking a pen from a colleague's desk can appear aggressive. Keep your distance; each of us has an 'egg-shaped' personal space which we defend when we feel aggrieved. Give everyone room to breathe.

Learn a clear communication technique

If you are afraid of giving offence by speaking your mind or are hidebound by the conventional stereotype of subordinate acquaintance or traditional feminine submission, assertiveness training makes good sense and will help you deal with verbal abuse without causing further aggression – you will also learn to say 'No'.

Talk yourself out of problems; placate rather than provoke people who are focusing their aggression on you.

Walk away from real danger

Remember that aggression meeting aggression adds up to confrontation and potential violence.

Your primary aim should always be to GET AWAY.

Carry and learn how to use an alarm; it can be used as a deterrent. Also if you press it down firmly and throw it to one side, the continuing horrendous scream will divert most attackers and attract help.

It helps to know your environment, to be AWARE, ALERT and AVOID trouble. Defend yourself only if really necessary.

Recognize a threat

Your aim in an increasingly aggressive situation is to leave the scene if possible. On the other hand if it is not possible or the situation demands it, you may decide it is necessary to mediate, to defuse or deal with a problem.

Your own anxiety is a better indicator of a potential threat than looking for signs of anxiety in others.

Anxiety is information for you to use – therefore, if the hair stands on end up the back of your neck, stop and assess. It may be more than just a natural reaction to change or the unknown.

Respond to difficult situations

Develop skills to defuse situations – or at least be able to prevent them from becoming more explosive – and to deal with those which are, or will be, actually violent. The use of physical restraint is a last resort only when there is real danger.

Protect yourself from physical attack
Self-defence is legally allowed only in certain circumstances. If you are attacked you have three options:

Attack   Flight   Compromise

It is safer for you to choose the last two!

Never walk deliberately into trouble to test your abilities. In any violent physical contact, everyone will be hurt.

Also, beware of being so confident that you do not take care.

Now make your own action plan. Use the blank page to write down what you intend to do and then go on to list the practical things you can personally do to avoid putting yourself at risk, at home, travelling out and about, and at work.

We all need to aim to be able to have the automatic responses made by a remarkable lady I once met on my travels:

She was the wife of a prison governor and her husband was called away to a meeting at the Home Office. Having got undressed, she got into bed, turned out the light, and was just tucking in the sheets when she put her hand down into a hand 'that was not her own'. 'Good heavens,' she said as she did so, 'that doesn't feel like a hand I know.'

Then she turned the light on, bent down and said in her most wonderful Scottish voice, 'Would you like a cup of tea?' The man came out and said with a sigh, 'Yes, I would. I've been here a very long time.' He was, of course, a very disturbed man and the talk went on until the early hours. Not many of us could have dealt with that situation in that kind of way. Experience and practice are essential aids to maturity. But the message is clear: surprise, especially if it is non-shocked and non-threatening, disarms aggression and works wonders.

A word of reassurance

The average person's chance of becoming a victim of any kind are very low – your chances of being attacked are once in a hundred years! But lesser troubles and aggravation come to us all more often and can cause much anguish as well as impaired work and absenteeism.

However, some of us have work that forces us to face more problematic situations, or may live in a difficult area. All these precautions which have been discussed in this book can reduce the risks we take.

They are commonsense, not difficult to follow and worthwhile if only to alleviate the fear of fear.

Protecting yourself is as straightforward as ABC:

Anxiety	–	Anticipation
Preventing Problems	–	Body Language
Communication	–	Confidence

As I say to everyone when we leave each other, 'Take care'; the Trust's concern is the care of people, we care that you 'Take care' – please do!

Personal Action Plan

List the practical things you personally can do to avoid putting yourself at risk:

At Home

Travelling out and about

At work

Further Information

Personal Safety

A Living Agenda – Report of a Conference on 'Aggression in the Workplace' available from SLT.

SLT leaflets can be obtained free from:
The Suzy Lamplugh Trust, 14, East Sheen Avenue, London, SW14 8AS.

Please send A5 s.a.e. If large quantities are needed please send postage and packing and a donation would be appreciated.

Various Home Office leaflets offering advice on safety and security – available from The Home Office, 50 Queen Anne's Gate, London SW1H 9AT.

Which – November 1990, Nos. 606, 636.

The Environment

Crime on the London Underground – HMSO, PO Box 276, London SW8 5DT.

Safer Cities – Progress Report 1989–1990, – Safer Cities Unit, Room 583a, The Home Office, 50 Queen Anne's Gate, London SW1H 9AT.

Report of the Working Group, Home Office Standing Committee for Violence on the Fear of Crime, Public Relations Branch, Room 133 Home Office, 50 Queen Anne's Gate, London SW1H 9AT.

Also available from the Home Office: *The 1988 British Crime Survey* – Home Office Research Study No.11.

Commissioner of Metropolis Report, 1989.

Secured by Design – Police Crime Prevention Scheme.

Fear of Crime – Home Office Report, 1989.

Local Authorities

The Essentials of Security Lighting – Electricity Publications, 30 Millbank, London SW1.

Registration of Private Hire Cars (Mini-Cabs) – Discussion paper from the Ministry of Transport, supported by The Trust – April 1989.

Neighbourhood Watch Schemes – Crime Concern, Level 8, David Murray John Building, Brunel Centre, Swindon SN1 1LY.

Lighting and Crime Prevention for Community Safety by Kate Painter – The Tower Hamlets Study 1st Report, Middlesex Polytechnic, 1989.

Dealing with Violence Procedure for Staff, South Staffordshire District Council, Council Offices, Codsall, Wolverhampton WV8 1PX.

The Media

A draft code of practice for television, radio and video works (including Cable TV) was presented by the Broadcasting Standards Council – February 1989. The Council was established by the Government to consider violence, sex, taste and decency in broadcasting and video works. The Chairman, Lord Rees Mogg, was appointed in May 1988.

Employees

Avoiding Danger – video available from the National Association of Citizen's Advice Bureaux, 115–123 Pentonville Road, London N1 9LZ.

Beating Aggression, a practical guide for working women by Diana Lamplugh, published by Weidenfeld & Nicolson.

You Can Cope – Suzy Lamplugh Trust training film – Gower Publications, Gower House, Croft Road, Aldershot, Hants GU11 3HR.

Smart Moves – Brook Street's video plus booklet – contact Clarence House, 134 Hatfield Road, St Albans, Herts AL1 4JB.

Coping with Confidence – Suzy Lamplugh Trust Training Consultancy.

Reducing the Risks booklet – free with s.a.e. (A5) – Suzy Lamplugh Trust (produced with the help of British Telecom).
Surveying Sisters – Women in a Traditional Male Profession by Clare Greed – Routledge 1991.

Victims
Criminal Injuries Compensation Board – Blythswood House, 200 Regent Street, Glasgow G2 4SW.
Rape Crisis Centre – see local telephone book.
Victim's Charter – copies available from The Home Office, 50 Queen Anne's Gate, London SW1H 9AT.
Victim Support – check local number with the Citizen's Advice Bureau.
Someone is Missing – Someone is Left Behind – Suzy Lamplugh Trust leaflet for the relatives and friends of Missing People – produced with the Woolwich Building Society.

Travel
The Highway Code – HMSO, P.O. Box 276, London SW8 5DT.
Travelwise – A series of Suzy Lamplugh Trust leaflets.
Mini-Cab Code and Safety Tips – in association with the Department of Transport.
Travelling Safely on Public Transport – in association with the Department of Transport.
Travelling Safely on Your Own – in association with the RAC.

Education
Junior Crime Panels – *Crime Prevention News*, Room 137, The Home Office, Queen Anne's Gate, London SW1H 9AT.
Stranger Danger Campaign – *Crime Prevention News*.
Kidscape and Teenscape – Crime Concern, Distribution Dept., Health Education Authority, Hamilton House, Mabledon Place, London WC1.
Well Safe booklet for teenagers – Suzy Lamplugh Trust.
A Handbook of Good Practice leaflet by J. Findlay, J. Gright and K. Gill – Crime Concern, Level 8, David Murray John Building, Brunel Centre, Swindon SN1 1LY.
Youth Action Against Vandalism leaflet – Crime Concern.

The Police

Practical Ways to Crack Crime handbook – Central Office of Information, Hercules Road, London SE1 7DU.

Positive Steps – video produced by Signet Films, available from the Metropolitan Police Library, MS8(1), Room 1326, New Scotland Yard, Broadway, SW1.

Crime Prevention Panels (local) – Crime Concern.

Secured by Design – police national crime prevention scheme to improve security of new homes – contact the Home Office.

The Employers

Preventing Violence to Staff – Payne and Harne, Tavistock Institute – HMSO.

The Cost of Violence – Seminar Report – Local Government Training Board.

Violence and Aggression in the Workplace – Health and Safety Executive booklet of guidelines for employers – free from the HSE, Baynards House, 1 Chepstow Place, London W2 4TF.

The Risks in Going to Work – C. M. Phillips, J. E. Stockdale and L. M. Joeman – Suzy Lamplugh Trust 1989.

Guidelines and Recommendations to Employers on Violence Against Employees – Association of Directors of Social Services 1987, Stockport MBC, Town Hall, Stockport SK1 3XE.

Violence to Staff: A Basis for Assessment and Prevention by B. Poyner & C. Narne – Health & Safety Executive, 1986. Contact HSE, Baynards House, 1 Chepstow Place, London W2 4TF.

Violence at Work: Issues, Policies and Procedures – C. M. Phillips, J. E. Stockdale – Local Government Management Board, Arndale House, Arndale Centre, Luton LU1 2TS.